Knitted & felted children's clothes

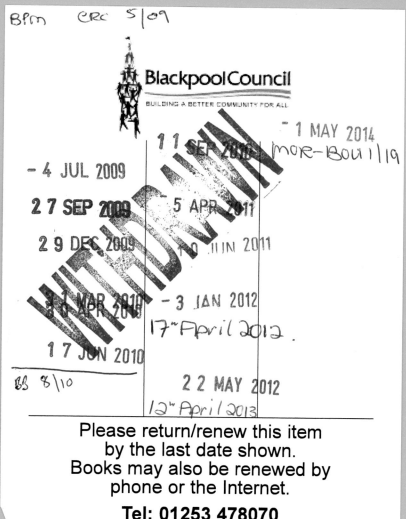

Knitted & felted children's clothes

22 delightful designs for tops, hats, scarves and bags

ZOË HALSTEAD

NH
NEW
HOLLAND

This book is dedicated to the children who inspired me:
Ellie and Blythe Lyons, George and James Foster and Elliot and Leo Halstead.

First published in 2009 by New Holland Publishers (UK) Ltd
London · Cape Town · Sydney · Auckland

Garfield House, 86–88 Edgware Road, London W2 2EA,
United Kingdom
www.newhollandpublishers.com

80 McKenzie Street, Cape Town 8001, South Africa
Unit 1, 66 Gibbes Street, Chatswood, NSW 2067, Australia
218 Lake Road, Northcote, Auckland, New Zealand

ISBN 978 1 84773 288 0

Senior Editor: **Clare Sayer**
Production: **Laurence Poos**
Design: **Lisa Tai**
Photography: **Sian Irvine**
Charts: **Stephen Dew**
Editorial Direction: **Rosemary Wilkinson**

10 9 8 7 6 5 4 3 2 1

Reproduction by Colourscan, Singapore
Printed and bound by Craft Print Pte Ltd, Singapore

Contents

Introduction

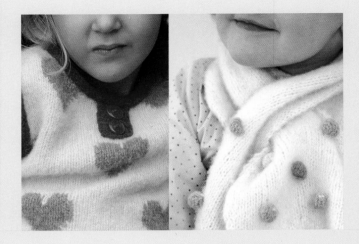

Having been a passionate hand knitter for more than 30 years I have always enjoyed knitting for children. Results are quick and I loved nothing more than creating a favourite knit for a new arrival or family member.

Since the arrival of my own sons, I am constantly disappointed by the uninspiring knitwear offered on the high street and so leapt at the chance to design the kind of funky, fresh knits I like to see on my own kids. Designing for children is always fun as I can indulge my love of wonderful colours, quirky details and fun themes.

This book is a collection of 22 inspiring designs for clothes and accessories for boys and girls. Two thirds of the knits have been made from felted knitting and there are full instructions on how to felt on pages 13–15. Felted knitting lends itself so perfectly to children's knitwear as the process produces a dense, hard wearing and resilient fabric for the toughest of kids. Garments knitted from wool lose all potential to be itchy and scratchy and are magically transformed into soft and fluffy clothes that children like wearing. There are a variety of felted projects here to suit all

tastes, from the cute Jurassic jacket and Sweetie cardigan; the covetable Fiesta bag and scarf and Bobble wrap with their felted pom poms; to the fun filled Tufty and 'Let it snow' hat and mittens.

There is also a collection of non felted designs which concentrate on smooth cotton, bamboo and vibrant coloured yarns as a contrast to the felted knits and include; a Pirate hat boys will love; the pretty Flowers and lace cardigan and the beautifully coloured, alpaca Fairisle scarf. Beautiful photographs of the children show each item in detail.

Each set of instructions includes all the information you will need to complete the project, along with a useful skill level indicator; from easy to advanced, to appeal to a broad spectrum of knitters.

I hope you have as much fun knitting, creating and felting these designs as I did thinking them up.

happy knitting and felting!

Getting started

The pages that follow contain all the information you will need to help you create beautiful knitted and felted clothes and accessories, from yarns and equipment to basic techniques.

KNITTED FABRICS

All knitted fabrics are made using just two basic stitches, knit and purl.

STOCKING STITCH (st st)

This is the most widely used knitted fabric. Alternate rows are knitted, the others are purled. With the knit side as the right side, the fabric is smooth and flat. With the purl side as the right side (referred to as reverse stocking stitch) the fabric has horizontal ridges. Stocking stitch will curl at the edges, however, the felting process usually helps to alleviate this and flatten the edges.

MOSS STITCH (moss st)

This is a textured stitch made up of alternate knit and purl stitches. Stitches that are knitted on one row will be knitted again on the next row. Stitches that are purled on one row will, again, be purled on the next. This produces a reversible, textured fabric that does not curl at the edges.

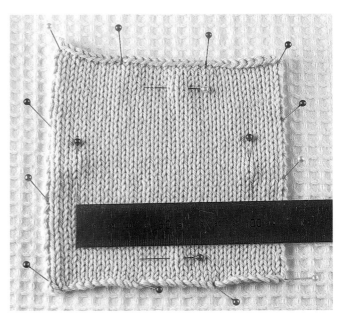

Checking tension

TENSION

For each pattern there is a recommended tension/gauge. It can seem like a chore to have to knit a tension square but it is extremely important, particularly with garments, if the finished item is to be correct for size.

Before starting a project, knit a tension square 5–10 more

stocking stitch

moss stitch

stitches and 5–10 more rows than stated in the tension note. Lay the finished square on a flat surface and smooth out, taking care not to distort the stitches. Using pins as markers, pin vertically between stitches and horizontally between rows, using a ruler or metal tape measure to measure 10 cm (4 in) square. Count the number of stitches and rows between the markers. If you have more stitches and rows than is stated in the tension note, you are knitting too tightly and you will need to try again with needles that are one size larger. If you have too few stitches and rows you are knitting too loosely and you will need to try again with needles that are one size smaller. Once you have achieved the correct tension your item will be knitted to the measurements given at the beginning of each pattern.

NEEDLES AND OTHER EQUIPMENT

Knitting needles are available in a variety of materials from aluminium to wood, and come in sizes ranging from 2 mm to 10 mm and beyond. They also come in a variety of lengths – what you use depends on personal preference. Whilst knitting and making up projects, you will also find the following equipment useful: a tape measure, safety pins, stitch holders, bobbins for colour knitting, scissors, pins and tapestry needles for sewing seams.

KNITTING NEEDLE CONVERSION TABLE

Metric	UK	US
2 mm	14	0
2¼ mm	13	1
2¾ mm	12	2
3 mm	11	2/3
3¼ mm	10	3
3¾ mm	9	5
4 mm	8	6
4½ mm	7	7
5 mm	6	8
5½ mm	5	9
6 mm	4	10
6½ mm	3	10½
7 mm	2	10½
7½ mm	1	11
8 mm	0	11
9 mm	00	13
10 mm	000	15

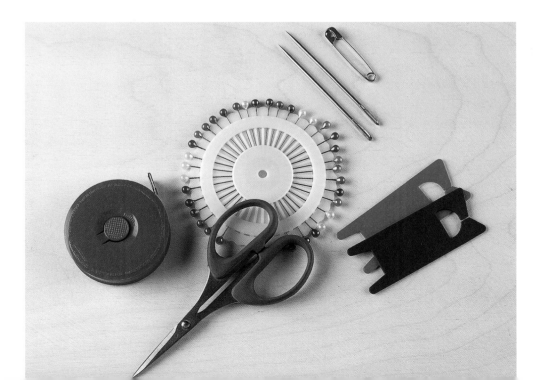

Examples of equipment you will find useful.

ABBREVIATIONS

The following are the general abbreviations used in the patterns:

alt	alternate	rem	remain(ing)
beg	begin(ning)	rep	repeat
ch	chain stitch (crochet)	rev st st	reverse stocking stitch
cm	centimetres	rnd	round
cont	continu(e)(ing)	RH	right hand
dec	decreas(e)(ing)	RS	right side
foll	following	skpo	slip 1, knit 1, pass slipped stitch over
folls	follows	sl (1)	slip (one stitch)
g st	garter stitch (k every row)	st(s)	stitch(es)
in	inch(es)	st st	stocking stitch (RS row k, WS row p)
inc	increase(e)(ing)	tbl	through back of loop(s)
k	knit	tog	together
LH	left hand	WS	wrong side
m1	make one, by picking up the bar in between this stitch and the next and working into the back of it	yb	yarn back
		yfwd	yarn forward
		yon	yarn over needle
meas	measures	yrn	yarn round needle
mm	millimetres	*	repeat instructions between asterisks as many times as instructed
patt	pattern		
p	purl	[ ]	work instructions inside as many times as instructed
psso	pass slipped stitch over		

COLOUR KNITTING

There are two main methods of working different colours in knitted fabric: intarsia and fairisle. The intarsia technique is usually used where a block of colour is required in just one area of the row, and there is usually a chart to follow for this. The fairisle technique is used when a pattern is repeated across the row, working different colours a few stitches at a time. Sometimes this is written as instructions, sometimes there is a chart to follow.

INTARSIA

For the intarsia technique it is best to have small lengths, balls or bobbins of yarn for each area of colour along the row. This produces a single thickness of fabric and the yarn is not carried across the back of the knitting so that the motif does not become distorted. Join in the various colours at

intarsia right side of fabric

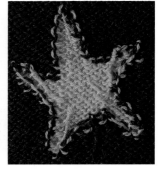

intarsia wrong side of fabric

the appropriate point in the row, and to avoid gaps in the knitting as you change colour, twist the yarns around each other on the wrong side. All ends can then be darned in at the end or knitted in as you work.

fairisle – right side of fabric

fairisle – wrong side of fabric

FAIRISLE

With the fairisle technique, the yarns are carried across the back and used every few stitches to form a repeating pattern (this is used in the Fairisle Scarf, see page 40). If the yarn has to carry over more than 3 stitches it's best to catch it in at the back, with the yarn you're knitting with at the time, to avoid long loops on the reverse. Try not to pull the yarns too tightly, as this will distort the fabric.

CHARTS

Some of the patterns in the book contain charts for colour knitting. Each square on the chart represents one stitch and each line of squares represents one row of knitting. When working from the charts, read odd rows (K) from right to left and even rows (P) from left to right. Each colour used is given a different symbol and these are shown in the key alongside each chart.

KEY

▲   cream 1A

☐   red 1403

YARNS

Each yarn in this book has been chosen as the best for each particular item. However, please do experiment with different colour ways and combinations to ring the changes in any of the designs. If you do substitute different yarn types, please be sure to knit a tension square to make sure you are happy with the different effect it may produce. Also, it is always best to substitute yarns with a similar meterage/yardage, so that the resulting knit is as close as possible to the original design.

YARN INFORMATION

YARNS FOR PLAIN KNITTING

Rowan Calmer: a lofty, soft, medium weight yarn (75% Cotton, 25% Acrylic/Microfibre). Approximately 160 m (175 yd) per 50 g (1¾ oz) ball.

RYC Cashsoft Baby DK: a soft, double knitting yarn (57% Extra Fine Merino, 33% Microfibre, 10% Cashmere). Approximately 130 m (142 yd) per 50 g (1¾ oz) ball.

Sirdar Snuggly Baby Bamboo DK: a double knitting yarn (80% Bamboo, 20% Wool). Approximately 95 m (103 yd) per 50 g (1¾ oz) ball.

Sirdar Click DK: a double knitting yarn (70% Acrylic, 30% Wool). Approximately 150 m (164 yd) per 50 g (1¾ oz) ball.

Sirdar Luxury Soft Cotton DK: a 100% Cotton double knitting yarn. Approximately 95 m (103 yd) per 50 g (1¾ oz) ball.

UK Alpaca Super Fine Dyed Colour Yarn: a double knitting yarn (70% Super Fine Alpaca, 30% British Bluefaced Leicester Wool). Approximately 132 m (145 yd) per 50 g (1¾ oz) ball.

YARN WEIGHT CONVERSION TABLE

UK	US
4 ply	Sport
Double knitting	Light worsted
Aran	Fisherman/Worsted
Chunky	Bulky
Super Chunky	Extra Bulky

YARNS FOR FELTED KNITTING

Jamieson & Smith (Shetland Wool Brokers) 2 ply Jumper Weight: a 100% Pure Shetland Wool yarn equivalent to 4 ply. Approximately 118 m (129 yd) per 25 g (1 oz) ball.

Rowan Scottish Tweed 4 ply: a 100% Pure New Wool 4 ply yarn. Approximately 110 m (120 yd) per 25 g (1 oz) ball.

Rowan Scottish Tweed DK: a 100% Pure New Wool double knitting yarn. Approximately 113 m (123 yd) per 50 g (1¾ oz) ball.

Twilleys of Stamford Freedom Spirit: a 100% Wool double knitting yarn. Approximately 120 m (131 yd) per 50 g (1¾ oz) ball.

Twilleys of Stamford Freedom Wool: a 100% Wool chunky yarn. Approximately 50 m (54 yd) per 50 g (1¾ oz) ball.

UK Alpaca Super Fine Natural Colour Yarn: a double knitting yarn (70% Super Fine Alpaca, 30% British Bluefaced Leicester Wool). Approximately 132 m (145 yd) per 50 g (1¾ oz) ball.

Felting information

As you will notice, over half of the items in this book have been made from knitting that has been felted. Traditionally, the term "felting" is only applied to raw, carded wool which is washed with soap and water to form a fluffy, dense, matted fabric. When the same process is applied to knitted fabric it is called "fulling". Wool fibres are made up of tiny scales that when exposed to hot water open up and expand or full. Combined with agitation and soap the fibres rub against each other and become meshed into a fluffy resilient fabric. Fulled fabric, therefore, is more dense, soft and warm to wear as it is less penetrable than ordinary knitted fabric. For the purposes of this book, however, I shall continue to refer to the process as felting.

YARNS

Most 100% wool, alpaca, mohair or animal fibre blends will felt well. However, it is best to avoid any 100% wool yarns that are labelled "machine washable" or "super wash" as these have been chemically treated so that the fibres will not burst or matt however roughly treated. Also, certain colours, including white and heather mixtures, felt much less quickly than others, if at all.

TENSION

For all of the felted knits in this book you will notice that the tension is deliberately loose. Generally speaking the needles are 2 mm larger than normally required to allow for the shrinkage that will occur when the knitting is felted. Most knitted pieces will shrink much more in length, usually by about a third, than in width and, as much as possible, this has been accounted for. However, every yarn (and sometimes every colour of the same yarn!) will react differently and that is why it is so important to do plenty of tension swatch knitting. I know it can seem like a chore to have to knit and then felt a tension swatch, but it can save you from some very costly mistakes. These swatches will give you a valuable insight into how the yarn will perform but please remember that larger

MAKING FELTED SWATCHES

These three swatches illustrate the felting process. All were knitted using Jamieson & Smith (Shetland Wool Brokers ltd) 2 ply Jumper Weight yarn and 3¾ mm (UK 9/US 5) needles at 35 sts and 50 rows.

Swatch 1
Before washing:
Measures 15.5 cm (6 in) wide by 16.5 cm (6.5 in) high.
Marked area of 10 cm (4 in) = 23 sts and 32 rows.

Swatch 2
After first wash Method A:
Measures 15 cm (6 in) wide by 13.75 cm (5.25 in) high.
10 cm (4 in) = 24 sts and 39 rows.
Marked area now measures 10 cm (4 in) wide by 8.5 cm (3.25 in) high

Swatch 3
After second wash Method A:
Measures 13.5 cm (5.25 in) wide by 12.5 cm (5 in) high.
10 cm (4 in) = 26 sts and 42 rows.
Marked area now measures 9 cm (3.5 in) wide by 7.5 cm (3 in) high

pieces can react differently. If you can, buy an extra ball of yarn in order to knit tension swatches for felting experiments, as once a swatch has been felted you can't then unravel the knitting to use for the main project! You can always use these felted swatches to make purses and mobile phone cases or cut them up into flower and heart shapes to decorate clothing.

Knit a tension square 5–10 more stitches and 5–10 more rows than stated in the tension note and then mark the 10 cm (4 in) square area with markers made from a yarn that will not felt (e.g. cotton). In this way, after washing, you will clearly be able to see how much shrinkage has occurred over the area without having to try and count stitches and rows that have become blurred by felting. Use the before and after notes provided in the tension details for each set of instructions to determine whether you have achieved the desired level of felting. It is particularly important that these tension notes are followed for garments that need to fit a certain size but less crucial for bags and scarves.

METHOD

There are two main ways of felting knitted fabric; either in the washing machine or by hand.

Felting by hand allows you to control the level to which your knitting is felted and therefore allows you to stop when you reach the desired level. It is hard work with garment sized pieces but good for small items like flowers which sometimes don't receive enough agitation in the washing machine.

Felting by machine takes out all of the hard work of hand felting and there's no risk of scalding! All of the felted knits in this book have been felted in my 12-year-old front loading washing machine in a hard water area, but if you have a top loading washing machine you may find machine felting even easier. You will be able to periodically stop the wash cycle and fish out your knitted pieces to check on their progress, continuing until you are happy with the results. However, most of the felting projects in this book required a full wash cycle – sometimes two or three in my machine to reach the correct level of felting. The number and length of your wash cycles and the results you achieve will depend on a variety of factors (including your machine's agitation process and whether you

have hard or soft water) which is why the tension swatch experiments are so important in assessing the best method for you.

The following are the main methods I used to achieve the felted knits in this book.

HOW TO FELT KNITTING IN THE WASHING MACHINE

You will need:
- Knitted pieces with all the ends sewn in.
- Soap rather than detergent; it can be liquid or flakes but look for 'soap' on the label.
- Agitators – dolly balls, jeans or an item of clothing that will withstand being washed at high temperatures (not towels as the lint transfers).
- Mesh laundry bags of the kind used to protect delicate items and keep small items safe. Available in various sizes.
- Washing machine
- Towel for drying.

METHOD A

1 Place a good handful of soap flakes or liquid directly in the washing machine drum. Place all the knitted pieces for the project in on top, placing small items such as pom poms in appropriate sized mesh bags and add the agitators.

2 Select the lowest water setting (half load button if you have one), the roughest agitation ('soiled' or 'main wash' setting) and 60°C temperature.

3 When the cycle has finished (this takes about 1½ hours in my machine), remove the knitted pieces and gently tease the matted edges apart and reshape.

TIP FOR METHOD A

Some of the item instructions call for this wash process to be repeated to achieve the correct felted tension. If you need to do this, it is important to let the knitted pieces dry thoroughly between washes otherwise the knitting becomes water logged and the pieces can grow rather than shrink.

4 Squeeze out any excess water by rolling the pieces in a towel.

5 Allow to air dry supported on a towel, out of direct sunlight.

METHOD B

1 Place a good handful of soap flakes or liquid directly in the washing machine drum. Place all the knitted pieces for the project in on top, placing small items such as pom poms in appropriate sized mesh bags and add the agitators.

2 Select the lowest water setting (half load button if you have one), medium agitation ('normal' or 'quick wash' setting) and 40°C temperature.

3 Wash for about 20 minutes then stop the machine, pump out the water and spin. Remove the knitted pieces and assess the level of felting. If all is satisfactory gently tease the matted edges apart, and reshape. If further felting is required repeat the process washing for 10 minute intervals before checking results.

4 Wash out any excess soap in the knitting by rinsing in lukewarm water. Squeeze out the water by rolling the pieces in a towel.

5 Allow to air dry supported on a towel, out of direct sunlight.

METHOD C

As Method B but this time select 60°C temperature setting.

HOW TO FELT KNITTING BY HAND

You will need:

- Knitted pieces with all the ends sewn in
- Soap rather than detergent, it can be liquid or flakes, but look for 'soap' on the label
- Two large shallow bowls (or sink and a large bowl)
- Pair of thick rubber gloves
- Hot and cold water
- Ice cubes
- Towel for drying

1 Fill your sink or a bowl with just boiled water and, wearing the rubber gloves, carefully add a handful of soap flakes or liquid and stir. Place the knitted pieces in the water and leave completely covered to soak for a few minutes.

GENERAL FELTING TIPS

Each pattern states which method of felting is required but this is based on my experience and machine. You will find out what works best for you as you get to know your machine and its capabilities through your swatch experiments. Felting is a variable process and how much you want to felt an item is up to you but please be aware that the more you felt the pieces the thicker they will become and the smaller the resulting item will be.

Felting knitting in a washing machine will produce a lot of fluff and lint. You may have to periodically wipe over the drum and door of your machine to remove this and it is a good idea to clean the filter on your washing machine regularly so as not to hamper future wash performance.

Some felting experts advocate sewing up seams on garments to be felted before they are washed. Because knitted fabric shrinks much more in length than width I find this can distort seams; for instance, where sleeves meet the armhole. I, therefore, only sew up small items such as flowers and leave everything else to be sewn up once felted.

2 Meanwhile, fill the other bowl with cold water and ice cubes.

3 Begin to knead, rub and agitate the knitted pieces vigorously in the hot water, taking care not to scald yourself.

4 Then switch to the cold water bowl and continue rubbing and agitating. Felting may happen quickly, or it may take several switches between the hot and the cold water.

5 Make sure to rub the piece evenly all over to retain the shape.

6 Keep the temperature of each bowl of water to its optimum level so that the knitting felts quickly.

7 When you have achieved your desired level of felting, rinse the pieces well. Squeeze out any excess water by rolling the pieces in a towel.

8 Allow to air dry supported on a towel, out of direct sunlight.

Making up and finishing

Please spend time finishing and making up well, as although the process can be time consuming, the resulting item will be a professional looking one.

PRESSING

When you have finished knitting all the pieces of your item, sew in all the yarn ends neatly.

All of the felted knitting pieces will not need to be pressed. For the plain knitted items, please refer to the ball band for pressing instructions.

BACKSTITCH

Unless otherwise stated, backstitch is good for sewing up the majority of the items in this book. With stripes and patterns, make sure to match the edges well.

Place the two pieces of knitting right sides together and pin in place. Thread a length of the correct coloured yarn into a large eyed, darning needle and secure it to the knitting where you want to begin stitching. Bring the needle up through both pieces of knitting, to the front one row up from the bottom of the knitting. Take the needle back down to the bottom edge and insert it, then bring it back up two

rows up from the bottom edge. Insert back in at the top of the first stitch and then back out two rows up. Continue in this way so that every stitch is one row down and two rows up, until the end of the seam. Fasten off.

Use the ridges and lines of the knitting to guide you so that your seams are kept straight.

MATTRESS STITCH

Use mattress stitch to join any seam where you want a particularly neat finish, as it produces a virtually invisible seam.

Thread a length of the correct coloured yarn into a large eyed darning needle and secure it to one piece of knitting where you want to begin stitching. Bring the needle to the front between the first and second stitches. Now lay both pieces of knitting to be joined with right sides facing you. Insert the needle between the first two stitches on the other piece and then again on the first piece. Keep stitching in this way, forming a neat zig zag of stitches between the two pieces and pulling the knitted pieces together every few stitches, until you reach the end of the seam. Fasten off.

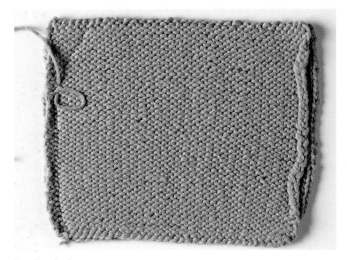

back stitch

mattress stitch

SAFETY
Please bear in mind the age of the recipient of each garment that you make. For young children make sure that buttons are sewn on securely so that they cannot become loose and be swallowed.

french knots

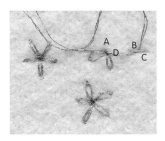
lazy daisy stitch

EMBROIDERY STITCHES

The following are the main embroidery stitches used.

LAZY DAISY STITCH

Bring the needle out at A. Insert back at A, and emerge at B, looping the yarn under the tip of the needle. Pull needle through and over loop and insert at C. Emerge at D for next stitch. Work a small stitch in the centre of the daisy once all the petals are completed.

FRENCH KNOTS

Bring the needle out at the required position. Hold the needle with your right hand and using your left hand wind the yarn around the tip of the needle about 3 times. Keeping the yarn in your left hand taut with the wraps on the needle, re-insert the needle a small distance away from where the yarn came up and pull the needle through to the reverse of the knitting, letting go of the yarn in your left hand. Try not to pull the needle through too hard otherwise the French knot will be pulled through to the wrong side of the knitting.

ADDITIONAL TECHNIQUES

Some of the items in this book require fringing and pom poms.

FRINGING

Cut the yarn to the required lengths. With the wrong side of the knitted fabric facing you, insert a crochet hook from the front to the back. Fold the yarn in half, place the loop on the hook and pull the loop of yarn through. Thread the ends of yarn through the loop and pull to make a knot against the

edge of the knitted fabric. Continue as per the instructions given for that particular item.

POM POMS

To make pom poms it is easiest to use one of the kits that are readily available. The kits usually contain plastic semi-circles or circles that clip together and allow you to wind your chosen yarn around. You then cut the yarn and remove the plastic parts to use again. Alternatively, you can use cardboard circles and make pom poms in the conventional way.

CARING FOR YOUR FINISHED GARMENT

For all of the plain knitted garments refer to the ball band for washing and drying instructions.

For felted garments; it is best to hand wash the garment and let it air dry, supported, out of direct sunlight. Try not to wash any of these garments in the washing machine, even on a wool cycle, as further shrinkage could occur.

fringing

pom pom

Poppy's beret and scarf

The yarn used for this design is a wonderful, soft, lofty one that is lovely to wear and a joy to knit with. The fresh colours make these pretty accessories for any little girl's outfit.

PLAIN KNITTING   SKILL LEVEL: **EASY**

MEASUREMENTS
Beret

Age	2–4	4–6	years
To fit head	51	53	cm
	20	21	in

Scarf (one size)

Actual length	105	cm
	41½	in

In the instructions, figures are given for the smaller size first; larger size follows in brackets. Where only one set of figures is given this applies to both sizes.

MATERIALS
- 2 x 50 g balls of Rowan Calmer in Pink/Coral 476
- 1 x 50 g ball of Rowan Calmer in Blue/Tinkerbell 475
- 1 x 50 g ball of Rowan Calmer in Green/Kiwi 485
- Pair each of 4 mm (UK 8/US 6) and 5 mm (UK 6/US 8) knitting needles

ABBREVIATIONS
See page 10

TENSION
21 sts and 30 rows to 10 cm (4 in) measured over stocking stitch using 5 mm (UK 6/US 8) needles.

BERET

With 4 mm (UK 8/US 6) needles and Pink cast on
100 (104) sts.
Beg with a k row, work 4 rows in st st.
Next row: P1, [k1, p1] to last st], k1.
Rep the last row 3 times more.
Change to 5 mm (UK 6/US 8) needles.

SET RIB PATTERN

Next row (RS): P4 (6), k2, [p8, k2] 9 times], p4 (6).
Next row (WS): K4 (6), p2, [k8, p2] 9 times], k4 (6).
Cont this patt throughout, keeping the ribs on the same sts
throughout, and shape as folls.
Next row (RS): P4 (6), k2, [p4, m1, p4, k2] 9 times], p4 (6).
(109 (113) sts.)
Work 3 rows incorporating new sts into patt.
Next row (RS): P4 (6), k2, [p5, m1, p4, k2] 9 times], p4 (6).
(118 (122) sts.)
Work 3 rows incorporating new sts into patt.
Next row (RS): P4 (6), k2, [p5, m1, p5, k2] 9 times], p4 (6).
(127 (131) sts.)
Work 3 rows incorporating new sts into patt.
Next row (RS): P4 (6), k2, [p6, m1, p5, k2] 9 times], p4 (6).
(136 (140) sts.)
Work 3 rows incorporating new sts into patt.

1st size only

Next row (RS): P1, m1, p2, m1, p1, k2, [p12, k2] 9 times],
p1, m1, p2, m1, p1. (140 sts.)
Work 1 WS row knitting new sts into patt.

2nd size only

Next row (RS): P3, m1, p3, k2, [p12, k2] 9 times], p3, m1,
p3. (142 sts.)
Work 1 WS row knitting new sts into patt.
Next row (RS): P4, m1, p3, k2, [p12, k2] 9 times], p3, m1,
p4. (144 sts.)
Work 1 WS row knitting new sts into patt.

Both sizes

SHAPE CROWN

Next row (RS): P6 (8), k2, [p5, p2tog, p5, k2] 9 times], p6
(8). (131 (135) sts.)
Work 1 WS row.
Next row (RS): P2 (3), p2tog, p2 (3), k2, [p5, p2tog, p4, k2]
9 times], p2 (3), p2tog, p2 (3). (120 (124) sts.)
Work 1 WS row.
Next row (RS): P5 (7), k2, [p4, p2tog, p4, k2] 9 times],
p5 (7). (111 (115) sts.)
Work 1 WS row.
Next row (RS): P2 (3), p2tog, p1 (2), k2, [p4, p2tog, p3, k2]
9 times], p2 (3), p2tog, p1 (2). (100 (104) sts.)
Work 1 WS row.
Next row (RS): P4 (6), k2, [p3, p2tog, p3, k2] 9 times],
p4 (6). (91 (95) sts.)
Work 1 WS row.
Next row (RS): P1 (2), p2tog, p1 (2), k2, [p3, p2tog, p2, k2]
9 times], p1 (2), p2tog, p1 (2). (80 (84) sts.)
Work 1 WS row.
Next row (RS): P3 (5), k2, [p2, p2tog, p2, k2] 9 times],
p3 (5). (71 (75) sts.)
Work 1 WS row.
Next row (RS): P1 (3), p2tog, k2, [p2, p2tog, p1, k2]
9 times], p1 (3), p2tog (60 (64) sts.)
Work 1 WS row.
Next row (RS): P2 (4), k2, [p1, p2tog, p1, k2] 9 times],
p2 (4). (51 (55) sts.)
Work 1 WS row.
Next row (RS): P2tog, p0 (2), k2, [p1, p2tog, k2] 9 times],
p2tog, p0 (2). (40 (44) sts.)
Work 1 WS row.
Next row (RS): P1 (3), k2, [p2tog, k2] 9 times], p1 (3).
(31(35) sts.)
Work 1 WS row.
Next row (RS): P1 (p2tog, p1), k2, [k2tog, k1] 9 times], p1
(p2tog, p1). (22 (24) sts.)
Work 1 WS row.

2nd size only
Next row (RS): P2tog, k20, p2tog. (22 sts.)
Work 1 WS row.
Both sizes
Next row (RS): P1, [k2tog] 10 times], p1. (12 sts.)
Work 1 WS row.
Next row (RS): P1, [k2tog] 5 times], p1. (7 sts.)
Break yarn (leaving a long length for making up), thread through rem 7 sts and draw up tightly.

SCARF

With 5 mm (UK 6/US 8) needles and Pink cast on 33 sts. Beg with a k row and working in st st stripes of 20 rows Pink, 20 rows Blue, 20 rows Green throughout, work until scarf measures 100 cm (39½ in) long approximately and 5 sets of stripe sequence have been worked. Work another 20 row Pink stripe to finish.
Cast off.

TO MAKE UP
BERET
Sew in all ends.
Sew centre back seam.
Make a large pom pom in Blue and sew to top of crown.
SCARF
Sew in all ends.
Sew each long edge together using mattress stitch, to form a tube. Place the seam at centre back.
Gather up each end of scarf.
Make 2 large pom poms in Blue and sew one to each end of scarf.

Tufty

This fun, tufted hat with cords and pom poms looks lovely bouncing around upon the heads of active kids. The bright colours and star motif suit both boys and girls.

FELTED KNITTING **SKILL LEVEL: MODERATE**

MEASUREMENTS

Age	2–4	4–6	years
To fit head	51	53	cm
	20	21	in
Actual width	50	53	cm
	20	21	in
Actual length	29	29	cm
	11½	11½	in

In the instructions, figures are given for the smaller size first; larger size follows in brackets. Where only one set of figures is given this applies to both sizes.

MATERIALS

- 1 (2) x 25 g balls of Jamieson & Smith (Shetland Wool Brokers Ltd) 2 ply Jumper Weight in Red 93
- 1 (2) x 25 g balls of Jamieson & Smith (Shetland Wool Brokers Ltd) 2 ply Jumper Weight in Turquoise 132
- 2 x 25 g balls of Jamieson & Smith (Shetland Wool Brokers Ltd) 2 ply Jumper Weight in Blue 18
- 1 x 25 g ball of Jamieson & Smith (Shetland Wool Brokers Ltd) 2 ply Jumper Weight in Yellow 91
- Pair each of 3¾ mm (UK 9/US 5) double pointed and 3¾ mm (UK 9/US 5) knitting needles

ABBREVIATIONS

See page 10

TENSION

Before machine felting:

23 sts and 32 rows to 10 cm (4 in) measured over stocking stitch using 3¾ mm (UK 9/US 5) needles.

After machine felting (Method A):

26 sts and 42 rows to 10 cm (4 in) measured over stocking stitch.

HAT

MAIN PIECE

With 3¾ mm (UK 9/US 5) needles and Red cast on
130 (138) sts.

Beg with a k row, work 22 rows in st st.

Change to Turquoise and beg with a k row, work 4 rows in
st st.

Change to Blue and beg with a k row, work 6 rows in st st.

PLACE STAR

Next row: K58 (62), k across 15 sts of first row of chart, k to
end.

Using the intarsia method, and beg with a p row, work the
rem 25 rows of the chart in st st. Cont in Blue.

KEY

| × | yellow |
| □ | blue |

SHAPE CROWN

Row 1: K14 (18), k2tog, [k31, k2tog] 3 times, k15 (19).
(126 (134) sts.)
P 1 row.

Row 3: K14 (18), k2tog, [k30, k2tog] 3 times, k14 (18).
(122 (130) sts.)
P 1 row.

Row 5: K14 (18), k2tog, [k29, k2tog] 3 times, k13 (17).
(118 (126) sts.)
P 1 row.

Row 7: K13 (17), k2tog, [k28, k2tog] 3 times, k13 (17).
(114 (122) sts.)
P 1 row.

Row 9: K13 (17), k2tog, [k27, k2tog] 3 times, k12 (16).
(110 (118) sts.)
P 1 row.

Row 11: K12 (16), k2tog, [k26, k2tog] 3 times, k12 (16).
(106 (114) sts.)
P 1 row.

Row 13: K12 (16), k2tog, [k25, k2tog] 3 times, k11 (15).
(102 (110) sts.)
P 1 row.

Row 15: K11 (15), k2tog, [k24, k2tog] 3 times, k11 (15).
(98 (106) sts.)
P 1 row.

Row 17: K11 (15), k2tog, [k23, k2tog] 3 times, k10 (14).
(94 (102) sts.)
P 1 row.

Row 19: K10 (14), k2tog, [k22, k2tog] 3 times, k10 (14). (90 (98) sts.)

P 1 row.

Row 21: K10 (14), k2tog, [k21, k2tog] 3 times, k9 (13). (86 (94) sts.)

P 1 row.

Row 23: K9 (13), k2tog, [k20, k2tog] 3 times, k9 (13). (82 (90) sts.)

P 1 row.

Row 25: K9 (13), k2tog, [k19, k2tog] 3 times, k8 (12). (78 (86) sts.)

P 1 row.

Row 27: K1, [k2tog] to last st, k1. (40 (44) sts.)

P 1 row.

Change to Turquoise.

Row 29: Inc twice in every st. (120 (132) sts)

P 1 row.

SHAPE TUFTS

* **Next row:** K4, turn.

Beg with a p row, work 31 rows in st st on these 4 sts only. Cast off. *

With RS facing rejoin yarn to rem sts and rep from * to * 29 (32) times more.

CORD

With 3¾ mm (UK 9/US 5) double pointed needles and Red, cast on 4 sts.

K 1 row.

Next row: ** Without turning the work, and RS facing, slide the sts to the other end of the needle and, pulling the yarn from the left hand side of the sts to the right across the back, k1 tbl, k3. **

Rep from ** to **, remembering to pull the yarn tightly across the back and always working a k row, until the cord meas 84 cm (33 in).

Cast off.

FELTING INSTRUCTIONS

Work in all ends with a needle.

Make 2 pom poms in Yellow approximately 5 cm (2 in) in diameter.

Following the instructions on page 14 for machine felting Method A, wash all pieces together, placing the pom poms and cord in a mesh laundry bag, to felt.

Reshape whilst damp, dry thoroughly and repeat wash cycle if necessary to achieve desired level of felting.

TO MAKE UP

With right sides together, stitch centre back seam. Turn right side out and gather up top just below turquoise tufts with running stitch and fasten off.

Sew a pom pom to each end of cord.

Wrap the cord around the hat just below and over the bottom of the tufts and tie. Sew to hat to secure.

Happy flappy

Cool denim stripes and ear flaps combine to keep the most active of boys warm and cosy. The tufted top adds a fun touch. To ring the changes in the colour way, why not use khaki greens?

FELTED KNITTING   **SKILL LEVEL: MODERATE**

MEASUREMENTS

Age	2–4	4–6	years
To fit head	51	53	cm
	20	21	in
Actual width	50	53	cm
	19½	21	in
Actual length	31	32	cm
(top of tufts to bottom	12	12½	in
of flaps)			

In the instructions, figures are given for the smaller size first; larger size follows in brackets. Where only one set of figures is given this applies to both sizes.

MATERIALS

- 1 x 25 g ball of Jamieson & Smith (Shetland Wool Brokers Ltd) 2 ply Jumper Weight in Dark Blue/Dark Denim FC47
- 1 x 25 g ball of Jamieson & Smith (Shetland Wool Brokers Ltd) 2 ply Jumper Weight in Light Blue/Light Denim FC15
- 1 x 25 g ball of Jamieson & Smith (Shetland Wool Brokers Ltd) 2 ply Jumper Weight in Medium Blue/Medium Denim FC37
- Pair each of 3¾ mm (UK 9/US 5) double pointed and 3¾ mm (UK 9/US 5) knitting needles

ABBREVIATIONS

See page 10

TENSION

Before machine felting:

23 sts and 32 rows to 10 cm (4 in) measured over stocking stitch using 3¾ mm (UK 9/US 5) needles.

After machine felting (Method A):

26 sts and 42 rows to 10 cm (4 in) measured over stocking stitch.

HAT

STRIPE SEQUENCE

Work 2 rows in Light Denim, 2 rows in Medium Denim, 2 rows in Light Denim, and 2 rows in Dark Denim. These 8 rows form the stripe pattern.

FRONT SECTION

With 3¾ mm (UK 9/US 5) needles and Dark Denim cast on 33 (39) sts.

* **Next row:** P1, [k1, p1] to end.
Next row: K1, [p1, k1] to end.
Rep the last 2 rows 3 times more.
Change to Light Denim and beg with a k row, work 22 rows in st st following the stripe sequence as set out above. *

SHAPE TOP

Cont in stripe sequence as set, dec 1 st at each end of next and every foll 4th row until 11 sts rem.
Beg with a p row, work 9 (1) row(s) in st st stripe sequence without shaping.
Cast off.

BACK SECTION

With 3¾ mm (UK 9/US 5) needles and Dark Denim cast on 19 (21) sts.
Work as for Front Section from * to *.

SHAPE TOP

Cont in stripe sequence as set, dec 1 st at each end of next and every foll 8th row until 5 (7) sts rem.
Beg with a p row, work 1 (5) row(s) in st st stripe sequence without shaping.
Cast off.

SIDE SECTION (Make 2)

With 3¾ mm (UK 9/US 5) needles and Light Denim cast on 7 sts.
Beg with a k row, work 2 rows in st st following the stripe sequence as set out above.

SHAPE FLAP

Cast on 3 sts at beg of next 2 rows. (13 sts.)
Inc 1 st at each end of next and every foll alt row to 39 sts.
Beg with a p row, work 31 rows in st st stripe sequence without shaping.

SHAPE TOP

Cont in stripe sequence as set, dec 1 st at each end of next and every foll 4th row until 11 sts rem.
P 1 row.
Cast off.

TUFTS

With 3¾ mm (UK 9/US 5) needles and Light Denim cast on 64 sts.

Beg with a k row, work 4 rows in st st.

** **Next row:** K4, turn.

Beg with a p row, work 19 rows in st st. on these 4 sts only. Cast off. **

With Medium Denim and RS facing, join yarn to rem sts and rep from ** to **.

With Light Denim and RS facing, join yarn to rem sts and rep from ** to **.

With Dark Denim and RS facing, join yarn to rem sts and rep from ** to **.

Cont in this way, rep the col sequence 3 more times and working 16 tufts altogether.

CORD

With 3¾ mm (UK 9/US 5) double pointed needles and Dark Denim, cast on 4 sts.

K 1 row.

Next row: *** Without turning the work, and RS facing, slide the sts to the other end of the needle and, pulling the yarn from the left hand side of the sts to the right across the back, k1 tbl, k3. ***

Rep from *** to ***, remembering to pull the yarn tightly across the back and always working a k row, until the cord meas 16 cm (6½ in).

Cast off.

FELTING INSTRUCTIONS

Work in all ends with a needle.

Following the instructions on page 14 for machine felting Method A, wash all pieces together, placing the Tufts and Cord in a mesh laundry bag, to felt.

Reshape whilst damp, dry thoroughly and repeat wash cycle if necessary to achieve desired level of felting.

TO MAKE UP

With right sides together join front and back sections to each side section with backstitch, making sure approximately 7.5 cm (3 in) of the side section protrudes

below the ribbed sections of the front and back to form ear flaps.

With right side facing and starting with the Light Denim tuft, roll the cast-on edge to form a coil with the Light Denim tuft at the centre, sewing through the layers as you go.

Place the tufted coil inside the top edge of the hat and sew in place.

Wrap the cord around the top edge of the hat to cover the cast-off edge and sew in place.

Blythe's beanie

A lace pattern that's surprisingly quick to knit combines with a knitted flower to produce a wonderfully sweet, soft hat. The lovely cashmere content of the yarn makes this a joy to knit.

PLAIN KNITTING

SKILL LEVEL: ADVANCED

MEASUREMENTS

Age	2–4	4–6	years
To fit head	51	53	cm
	20	21	in
Actual width	50	52	cm
	19½	20½	in
Actual length	20	21	cm
	8	8¼	in

In the instructions, figures are given for the smaller size first; larger size follows in brackets. Where only one set of figures is given this applies to both sizes.

MATERIALS

- 1 (2) x 50 g balls of RYC Cashsoft Baby DK in Pink/Pixie 807
- Pair of 3¾ mm (UK 9/US 5) knitting needles

ABBREVIATIONS

See page 10

TENSION

23 sts and 32 rows to 10 cm (4 in) measured over stocking stitch using 3¾ mm (UK 9/US 5) needles.

HAT

MAIN PIECE

With 3¾ mm (UK 9/US 5) needles and Pink cast on
115 (119) sts.

LACE PATTERN

Row 1: K2 (4), yrn, p5, p3tog, p5, yrn, [k1, yon, p5, p3tog,
p5, yon] to last 2 (4) sts, k2 (4).
Row 2: P to end.
Rep the last 2 rows 5 times more.
Row 13: K2 (4), yfwd, skpo, yrn, p3, p3tog, p3, yon, k2tog,
yrn, [k1, yfwd, skpo, yrn, p3, p3tog, p3, yon, k2tog, yfwd] to
last 2 (4) sts, k2 (4).
Row 14: And every alt row, p to end.
Row 15: K2 (4), yfd, k1, skpo, yrn, p2, p3tog, p2, yon,
k2tog, k1, yford, [k1, yfd, k1, skpo, yrn, p2, p3tog, p2, yon,
k2tog, k1, yfd] to last 2 (4) sts, k2 (4).
Row 17: K2 (4), yrn, k2, skpo, yrn, p1, p3tog, p1, yon,
k2tog, k2, yfwd, [k1, yfwd, k2, skpo, yrn, p1, p3tog, p1, yon,
k2tog, k2, yfwd] to last 2 (4) sts, k2 (4).
Row 19: K2 (4), yfwd, k3, skpo, yon, p3tog, yrn, k2tog, k3,
yfwd, [k1, yfwd, k3, skpo, yrn, p3tog, yon, k2tog, k3, yfwd]
to last 2 (4) sts, k2 (4).
Row 21: K5 (7), k2tog, yfwd, k3, yfwd, skpo, k3, [k4, k2tog,
yfwd, k3, yfwd, skpo, k3] to last 2 (4) sts, k2(4).
Row 23: K4 (6), k2tog, yfwd, k5, yfwd, skpo, k2, [k3, k2tog,
yfwd, k5, yfwd, skpo, k2] to last 2 (4) sts, k2 (4).
Row 25: K3 (5), k2tog, yfwd, k7, yfwd, skpo, k1, [k2, k2tog,
yfwd, k7, yfwd, skpo, k1] to last 2 (4) sts, k2 (4).
Row 27: K2 (4), k2tog, yfwd, k9, yfwd, skpo, [k1, k2tog,
yfwd, k9, yfwd, skpo,] to last 2 (4) sts, k2 (4).
Row 29: K1 (3), k2tog, yfwd, k11, [yfwd, [sl 2 sts, k1, psso,
yfwd, k11] to last 3 (5) sts, yfwd, skpo, k1 (3).
Beg with a p row, work 9 (13) rows in st st.

SHAPE CROWN

Row 1: K1 (3), skpo, [k12, skpo] 4 times, k11, [k2tog, k12]
3 times], k2tog, k1 (3). (106 (110) sts.)
P 1 row.
Row 3: K1 (3), skpo, [k11, skpo] 4 times, k9, [k2tog, k11]
3 times], k2tog, k1 (3). (97 (101) sts.)
P 1 row.
Row 5: K1 (3), skpo, [k10, skpo] 4 times, k7, [k2tog, k10]
3 times], k2tog, k1 (3). (88 (92) sts.)
P 1 row.
Row 7: K1 (3), skpo, [k9, skpo] 4 times, k5, [k2tog, k9]
3 times], k2tog, k1 (3). (79 (83) sts.)
P 1 row.
Row 9: K1 (3), skpo, [k8, skpo] 4 times, k3, [k2tog, k8]
3 times], k2tog, k1 (3). (70 (74) sts.)
P 1 row.
Row 11: K1 (3), skpo, [k7, skpo] 4 times, k1, [k2tog, k7]
3 times], k2tog, k1 (3). (61 (65) sts.)
P 1 row.
Row 13: K1 (3), skpo, [k6, skpo] 4 times, k7, [k2tog, k6]
twice], k2tog, k1 (3). (53 (57) sts.)
P 1 row.
Row 15: K1 (3), skpo, [k5, skpo] 3 times, k5, [k2tog, k5]
3 times], k2tog, k1 (3). (45 (49) sts.)
P 1 row.
Row 17: K1 (3), skpo, [k4, skpo] 3 times, k3, [k2tog, k4]
3 times], k2tog, k1 (3). (37 (41) sts.)
P 1 row.
Row 19: K1 (3), skpo, [k3, skpo] 3 times, [k2, k2tog] twice],
[k3, k2tog] twice], k1 (3). (29 (33) sts.)
P 1 row.
Row 21: K1 (3), skpo, [k2, skpo] 3 times], [k1, k2tog] twice],
[k2, k2tog] twice], k0 (2). (21 (25) sts.)
P 1 row.
Row 23: K1, [k2tog to end]. (11 (13) sts.)
P 1 row.
Row 25: K1, [k2tog to end]. (6 (7) sts.)
Break yarn, thread through rem sts and draw up tightly.

FLOWER CENTRE

With 3¾ mm (UK 9/US 5) needles and Pink cast on 35 sts.
Row 1: (RS) [K1, cast off 5 sts (2 sts left on RH needle)] to end. (10 sts.)
Break yarn, thread through rem sts and draw up tightly.

FLOWER

With 3¾ mm (UK 9/US 5) needles and Pink cast on 68 sts.
P 1 row.
Next row: K2, *k1, sl this st back onto LH needle, pass the next 8 sts over the top of this st and off the needle, [yrn] twice, k the sl st again, k2, rep from * to end.
Next row: P1, [p2tog, p1, p1 tbl, p1], to last st, p1.
Next row: [K2tog] to end. (13 sts.)
P1 row.
Next row: K1, [k2tog] to end]. (7 sts.)
Break yarn, thread through rem sts, pull up tightly and fasten off.

TO MAKE UP

Sew centre back seam using mattress stitch. Sew flower centre to the middle of the flower and then sew to the hat just above the lace pattern to the left of centre front.

Bobble wrap

The bobbles and pom poms on this softly coloured wrap are made all the more special by the felting process. The base of soft, fluffy cream is perfect to snuggle up to on cold wintry days.

FELTED KNITTING SKILL LEVEL: **MODERATE**

MEASUREMENTS
One size to fit ages **2–6 years**
Wrap Approximately 20 cm (8 in) wide
75 cm (29½ in) long

MATERIALS
- 3 x 25 g balls of Jamieson & Smith (Shetland Wool Brokers Ltd) 2 ply Jumper Weight in Cream 1A
- 1 x 25 g ball of Jamieson & Smith (Shetland Wool Brokers Ltd) 2 ply Jumper Weight in Blue/Pale Blue 14
- 1 x 25 g ball of Jamieson & Smith (Shetland Wool Brokers Ltd) 2 ply Jumper Weight in Pink/Rose 101
- 1 x 25 g ball of Jamieson & Smith (Shetland Wool Brokers Ltd) 2 ply Jumper Weight in Lilac 49
- 1 x 25 g ball of Jamieson & Smith (Shetland Wool Brokers Ltd) 2 ply Jumper Weight in Turquoise/Seafoam 75
- Pair of 5½ mm (UK 5/US 9) knitting needles

ABBREVIATIONS
MB = Make Bobble; see also page 10

TENSION
Before machine felting:
18 sts and 24 rows to 10 cm (4 in) measured over stocking stitch using 5½ mm (UK 5/US 9) needles.
After machine felting (method A):
20½ sts and 33 rows to 10 cm (4 in) measured over stocking stitch.

WRAP

MAKE BOBBLE (MB)
Join in col required.
Work into the front and back of the next st until there are 5 sts, turn.
Beg with a p row, work 4 rows in st st on these 5 sts only.
Next row: P2tog, p1, p2tog.
Next row: With Cream, k3tog, cont along row as instructions state.

WRAP
With 5½ mm (UK 5/US 9) needles and Cream cast on 45 sts.
Beg with a k row, work 12 rows in st st. *

BOBBLE PATTERN
Next row: K8, MB Blue, k13, MB Seafoam, k13, MB Lilac, k8.
Beg with a p row, work 9 rows in st st.
Next row: K15, MB Lilac, k13, MB Pink, k15.
Beg with a p row, work 9 rows in st st.
Next row: K8, MB Pink, k13, MB Blue, k13, MB Seafoam, k8.

Beg with a p row, work 9 rows in st st.

Next row: K15, MB Seafoam, k13, MB Lilac, k15.

Beg with a p row, work 9 rows in st st.

Next row: K8, MB Lilac, k13, MB Pink, k13, MB Blue, k8.

Beg with a p row, work 5 rows in st st.

DIVIDE FOR OPENING

Next row: K22, turn.

* Beg with a p row, work 21 rows in st st on these 22 sts only.*

Leave these sts on a holder.

With RS facing, rejoin yarn to rem sts and cont as follows.

Next row: Cast off 1 st, k to end. (22 sts.)

Work as for 1st side from * to *.

Leave these sts on a spare needle.

With RS facing rejoin yarn and k 22 sts from holder inc 1 in last st, and then 22 sts from spare needle. (45 sts.)

Beg with a p row, work 95 rows in st st ending with a p row.

BOBBLE PATTERN

Next row: K8, MB Lilac, k13, MB Pink, k13, MB Blue, k8.

Beg with a p row, work 9 rows in st st.

Next row: K15, MB Seafoam, k13, MB Lilac, k15.

Beg with a p row, work 9 rows in st st.

Next row: K8, MB Pink, k13, MB Blue, k13, MB Seafoam, k8.

Beg with a p row, work 9 rows in st st.

Next row: K15, MB Lilac, k13, MB Pink, k15.

Beg with a p row, work 9 rows in st st.

Next row: K8, MB Blue, k13, MB Seafoam, k13, MB Lilac, k8.

Beg with a p row, work 11 rows in st st.

Cast off.

POM POMS

Make pom poms measuring approximately 3.5 cm (1½ in) in diameter as follows:

Make 4 Cream pom poms, 2 Blue pom poms, 2 Pink pom poms, 2 Lilac pom poms and 2 Seafoam pom poms.

FELTING INSTRUCTIONS

Work in all ends with a needle.

Following the instructions on page 14 for machine felting Method A, wash all pieces together, placing the pom poms in mesh laundry bags, to felt.

Reshape whilst damp, dry thoroughly and repeat wash cycle if necessary to achieve desired level of felting.

TO MAKE UP

Sew pom poms along each end of the wrap in the following sequence:

Left edge, Seafoam, Lilac, Cream, Pink, Blue, Cream, right edge.

Fiesta bag and scarf

This beautiful bag and scarf set highlights the wonderful results you can achieve from felting pom poms. The zingy colours and fun texture are sure to be a winner and are so easy to produce.

FELTED KNITTING   SKILL LEVEL: **EASY** ★☆☆

MEASUREMENTS

One size	to fit ages **2–6 years**
Bag	Approximately 20 cm (8 in) square
Scarf	Approximately 12 cm (5 in) wide, 97 cm (38 in) long

Position guide for pom poms on bag and scarf

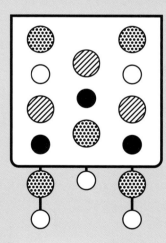

KEY
- ⬤ bright red
- ⬤ dark red
- ⬤ lilac
- ⬤ orange

MATERIALS

- 4 x 25 g balls of Jamieson & Smith (Shetland Wool Brokers Ltd) 2 ply Jumper Weight in Purple 20
- 1 x 25 g ball each of Jamieson & Smith (Shetland Wool Brokers Ltd) 2 ply Jumper Weight in Lilac 49, Bright Red 93, Orange 125 and Dark Red 1403
- Pair of 3¾ mm (UK 9/US 5) knitting needles
- 3¼ mm (UK 10/US D/3) crochet hook
- Fabric for lining bag 40 x 20 cm (15½ x 8 in)

ABBREVIATIONS

See page 10

TENSION

Before machine felting:

23 sts and 32 rows to 10 cm (4 in) measured over stocking stitch using 3¾ mm (UK 9/US 5) needles.

After machine felting (method A):

26 sts and 42 rows to 10 cm (4 in) measured over stocking stitch.

BAG

BACK & FRONT (worked as one piece)
With 3¾ mm (UK 9/US 5) needles and Purple cast on 52 sts.
Beg with a k row, work in st st until piece measures 52 cm
(21 in) from cast-on edge.
Cast off.

HANDLES (Make 2)
With 3¾ mm (UK 9/US 5) needles and Purple cast on 12 sts.
Beg with a k row, work in st st until piece measures 31 cm
(12½ in) from cast-on edge.
Cast off.

POM POMS
Make pom poms as follows:
5 small Lilac pom poms, 5 medium Bright Red pom poms,
3 medium Dark Red pom poms and 3 small Orange pom
poms.
Leave a long length of yarn attached to 2 of the medium
Bright Red pom poms and 3 of the small Lilac pom poms,
and using a 3¼ mm (UK 10/US D/3) crochet hook make
15 chain and fasten off.

SCARF

MAIN PIECE
With 3¾ mm (UK 9/US 5) needles and Purple cast on 32 sts.
Beg with a k row, work in st st until piece measures 124 cm
(48½ in) from cast-on edge.
Cast off.

POM POMS
Make pom poms as follows:
Make 4 medium Lilac pom poms, 2 medium and 2 small
Bright Red pom poms, 4 small Dark Red pom poms and
2 small and 2 medium Orange pom poms.
Leave along length of yarn attached to 1 medium Bright Red
pom pom, 1 small Bright Red pom pom, 2 small Dark Red

pom poms, 2 medium Lilac pom poms and 1 small and
1 medium Orange pom poms, and using a 3¼ mm
(UK 10/US D/3) crochet hook chain 15 and fasten off.

FELTING INSTRUCTIONS
Work in all ends with a needle.
Following the instructions on page 14 for machine felting
Method A, wash all pieces together, placing the pom poms
in mesh laundry bags, to felt.
Reshape whilst damp, dry thoroughly and repeat wash cycle
if necessary to achieve desired level of felting.

TO MAKE UP
BAG
Fold the bag piece in half widthways and sew the pom
poms to the front as the diagram shows. Using the chain
sections sew the pom poms to each other and to the
bottom folded edge of bag as diagram shows.
Sew side seams.
Roll the long edges of each handle piece towards each
other and sew.
Sew each handle inside the top edges of the front and
back of bag.
Cut a piece of lining fabric measuring 40 x 20 cm
(15½ x 8 in), fold in half widthways and sew the side seams.
Place inside the bag, wrong sides together and stitch to the
inside top edge all the way round.
SCARF
Sew pom poms to each end of scarf as diagram shows.
Using the chain sections sew the pom poms to each other
and to the bottom edges of scarf as diagram shows.

Fairisle scarf

Made from a luxury alpaca yarn in gorgeous, saturated colours, this scarf is lovely to wear and will be admired by many. Once mastered, the fairisle technique is easy to knit and produces wonderful results.

PLAIN KNITTING SKILL LEVEL: **MODERATE**

MEASUREMENTS

One size	to fit ages **2–6 years**
Scarf	Approximately 18 cm (7 in) wide, 140 cm (55 in) long

MATERIALS

- 2 x 50 g balls of UK Alpaca Super Fine Double Knit in **Rose Pink**
- 2 x 50 g balls of UK Alpaca Super Fine Double Knit in **Lilac**
- 1 x 50 g ball of UK Alpaca Super Fine Double Knit in **Sapphire Blue**

ABBREVIATIONS

See page 10

TENSION

25 sts and 34 rows to 10 cm (4 in) measured over stocking stitch using 3¾ mm (UK 9/US 5) needles.

SCARF

MAIN PIECE

With 3¾ mm (UK 9/US 5) needles and Rose Pink cast on 46 sts.

Beg with a k row, and using the Fairisle technique, work in st st following the chart.

The chart (see page 42) has a pattern repeat of 72 rows.

Work until the chart has been repeated 5 times (360 rows). Cast off.

TO MAKE UP

Sew in all ends.

Turn under each end of the scarf and slip stitch in place to form a narrow hem.

Cut 15 x 15 cm (6 in) lengths of Rose Pink, Lilac, and Sapphire Blue yarn. Divide the lengths into 15 groups of 1 length of each colour. Fold each group in half and loop through one end of the scarf to form a fringe.

Repeat at the other end of the scarf.

KEY

☐   Rose Pink

o   Lilac

×   Sapphire Blue

Let it snow hat and mittens

The red and cream colour way and snowflake design of this hat and mittens have a wonderful Scandinavian feel. As the name implies, it would make the perfect Christmas gift for an excitable youngster!

FELTED KNITTING   SKILL LEVEL: **MODERATE**

MEASUREMENTS

Age	2–5	years
HAT		
To fit head	51–53	cm
	20–21	in
Actual width	53	cm
	21	in
Actual length		
(front edge to top of tuft)	21	cm
	8	in
MITTENS		
Actual width		
(above thumb)	16.5	cm
	6½	in
Actual length	15	cm
	6	in

MATERIALS

- 3 x 25 g balls of Jamieson & Smith (Shetland Wool Brokers Ltd) 2 ply Jumper Weight in Red/Dark Red 1403
- 1 x 25 g ball of Jamieson & Smith (Shetland Wool Brokers Ltd) 2 ply Jumper Weight in Cream 1A
- Set of four 3¾ mm (UK 9/US 5) double pointed and a pair of 3¾ mm (UK 9/US 5) knitting needles

ABBREVIATIONS

See page 10

TENSION

Before machine felting:

23 sts and 32 rows to 10 cm (4 in) measured over stocking stitch using 3¾ mm (UK 9/US 5) needles.

After machine felting (Method A):

26 sts and 42 rows to 10 cm (4 in) measured over stocking stitch.

HAT

MAIN PIECE (worked in the round)

With 3¾ mm (UK 9/US 5) needles and Red cast on 130 sts.
Place markers at the 17th, 41st, 89th and 113th sts.
Divide the stitches between three double pointed needles,
so that you have 43 sts on two and 44 sts on the other.
Place marker at beg of rnd.
K 1 rnd.
P 1 rnd.
Rep the last 2 rnds once more. Then k 48 rnds.

SHAPE CROWN

Next rnd: K8, k2tog, [k14, k2tog] 7 times], k8. (122 sts.)
K 1 rnd.
Next rnd: K8, k2tog, [k13, k2tog] 7 times], k7. (114 sts.)
K 1 rnd.
Next rnd: K7, k2tog, [k12, k2tog] 7 times], k7. (106 sts.)
K 1 rnd.
Next rnd: K7, k2tog, [k11, k2tog] 7 times], k6. (98 sts.)
K 1 rnd.
Next rnd: K6, k2tog, [k10, k2tog] 7 times], k6. (90 sts.)
K 1 rnd.
Next rnd: K6, k2tog, [k9, k2tog] 7 times], k5. (82 sts.)
K 1 rnd.
Next rnd: K5, k2tog, [k8, k2tog] 7 times], k5. (74 sts.)
K 1 rnd.
Next rnd: K5, k2tog, [k7, k2tog] 7 times], k4. (66 sts.)
K 1 rnd.
Next rnd: K4, k2tog, [k6, k2tog] 7 times], k4. (58 sts.)
K 1 rnd.
Next rnd: K4, k2tog, [k5, k2tog] 7 times], k3. (50 sts.)
K 1 rnd.
Next rnd: K3, k2tog, [k4, k2tog] 7 times], k3. (42 sts.)
K 1 rnd.
Next rnd: K3, k2tog, [k3, k2tog] 7 times], k2. (34 sts.)
K 1 rnd.
Next rnd: K1, k2tog, k28, k2tog, k1. (32 sts.)
K 1 rnd.
Next rnd: [K2tog] 16 times. (16 sts.)

Next rnd: [K2tog] 8 times. (8 sts.)
K 11 rnds on these 8 sts only.
Next rnd: [K2tog] 4 times. (4 sts.)
Break yarn, thread through rem sts and draw up tightly.

LEFT EARFLAP

With RS of hat facing, 3¾ mm (UK 9/US 5) needles and Red,
pick up and k 23 sts between the markers at the 17th and
41st sts.
* P 1 row.

PLACE CHART

Next rnd: K2, k across 1st row of chart using the fairisle
method, k2.
Work a further 27 rows of chart.

SHAPE BOTTOM

Keeping chart correct as set, dec as follows.
Cast off 3 sts at beg of next 4 rows. (11 sts.)
Cast off rem 11 sts. *

RIGHT EARFLAP

With RS of hat facing, 3¾ mm (UK 9/US 5) needles and Red,
pick up and k 23 sts between the markers at the 89th and
113th sts.
Work as for Left Earflap from * to *.

KEY

▲ Cream 1A
☐ Red 1403

MITTENS

RIGHT MITTEN

** With 3¾ mm (UK 9/US 5) needles and Red, cast on 42 sts.

Next row: K1, [p1, k1] to last st], p1.
Rep the last row 9 times more. **

SHAPE THUMB

Next row: K23, [m1] twice], k19. (44 sts.)
P 1 row.
Next row: K23, m1, k2, m1, k19. (46 sts.)
P 1 row.

PLACE CHART

Next row: K2, k across 1st row of chart, k2, m1, k4, m1, k19. (48 sts.)
P 1 row, working 2nd row of chart.
Cont working from the chart and at the same time cont to shape thumb as follows.

Next row: K23, m1, k6, m1, k19. (50 sts.)
P 1 row.
Next row: K23, m1, k8, m1, k19. (52 sts.)
P 1 row.
Next row: K23, m1, k10, m1, k19. (54 sts.)
P 1 row.
Next row: K23, m1, k12, m1, k19. (56 sts.)
P 1 row.
Next row: K23, m1, k14, m1, k19. (58 sts.)
P 1 row.

DIVIDE FOR THUMB

Next row: K39 (cont chart), turn.
Next row: Cast on and p 1 st, p16, turn.
Next row: Cast on and k 1 st, k to end. (18 sts.)
*** Beg with a p row, work 15 rows in st st on these 18 sts only.
Next row: K1, [k2tog] to end. (10 sts.)
P 1 row.
Next row: [K2tog] to end. (5 sts.)
Break yarn (leaving a long length), thread through rem sts

and draw up tightly.

With RS facing, rejoin yarn to rem sts and pick up and k 2 sts from cast-on sts at base of thumb then k to end. (44 sts.)

Work rem 17 rows of chart.

Beg with a k row, work 4 rows in st st.

SHAPE TOP

Next row: [K1, skpo, k16, k2tog, k1] twice. (40 sts.)

P1 row.

Next row: [K1, skpo, k14, k2tog, k1] twice. (36 sts.)

P1 row.

Cont to dec in this way on every alt row (working 2 sts less between decs each time) until 12 sts rem.

P 1 row.

Cast off. ***

LEFT MITTEN

Work as for Right Mitten from ** to **.

SHAPE THUMB

Next row: K19, [m1] twice], k23. (44 sts.)

P 1 row.

Next row: K19, m1, k2, m1, k23. (46 sts.)

P 1 row.

PLACE CHART

Next row: K19, m1, k4, m1, k2, k across 1st row of chart, k2. (48 sts.)

P 1 row, working 2nd row of chart.

Cont working from the chart and at the same time cont to shape thumb as follows.

Next row: K19, m1, k6, m1, k23. (50 sts.)

P 1 row.

Next row: K19, m1, k8, m1, k23. (52 sts.)

P 1 row.

Next row: K19, m1, k10, m1, k23. (54 sts.)

P 1 row.

Next row: K19, m1, k12, m1, k23. (56 sts.)

P 1 row.

Next row: K19, m1, k14, m1, k23. (58 sts.)

P 1 row.

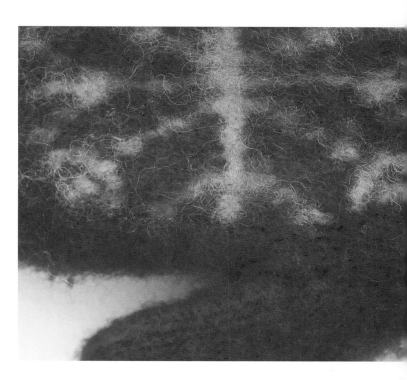

DIVIDE FOR THUMB

Next row: K35, turn.

Next row: Cast on and p 1 st, p16, turn.

Next row: Cast on and k 1 st, k to end. (18 sts.)

Work as for Right Mitten from *** to ***.

FELTING INSTRUCTIONS

Work in all ends with a needle.

With Cream, work French knots randomly all over crown of hat.

Sew thumb seam of mittens using mattress stitch before washing.

Following the instructions on page 14 for machine felting Method A, wash all pieces together to felt.

Reshape whilst damp, dry thoroughly and repeat wash cycle if necessary to achieve desired level of felting.

TO MAKE UP

Sew side and top seam of each mitten.

Groovy gloves

With their bright colours, spotty pattern and French knots; these fluffy gloves are bound to keep little hands warm and toasty and raise a smile in all who see them!

FELTED KNITTING **SKILL LEVEL: MODERATE**

MEASUREMENTS

Age	2–4	4–6	years
Actual width	16.5	18	cm approximately
(above thumb)	6½	7	in approximately
Actual length	16	17	cm approximately
(longest finger)	6	6½	in approximately

In the instructions, figures are given for the smaller size first; larger size follows in brackets. Where only one set of figures is given this applies to both sizes.

MATERIALS

- 1 x 25 g ball of Jamieson & Smith (Shetland Wool Brokers Ltd) 2 ply Jumper Weight in Green 79
- 1 x 25 g ball of Jamieson & Smith (Shetland Wool Brokers Ltd) 2 ply Jumper Weight in Indigo 131
- 1 x 25 g ball of Jamieson & Smith (Shetland Wool Brokers Ltd) 2 ply Jumper Weight in Red 93
- 1 x 25 g ball of Jamieson & Smith (Shetland Wool Brokers Ltd) 2 ply Jumper Weight in Yellow 91
- 1 x 25 g ball of Jamieson & Smith (Shetland Wool Brokers Ltd) 2 ply Jumper Weight in Blue 16
- Pair each of 3¼ mm (UK 10/US 3) and 3¾ mm (UK 9/US 5) knitting needles

ABBREVIATIONS

See page 10

TENSION

Before machine felting:
23 sts and 32 rows to 10 cm (4 in) measured over stocking stitch using 3¾ mm (UK 9/US 5) needles.

After machine felting (Method A):
26 sts and 42 rows to 10 cm (4 in) measured over stocking stitch.

GLOVES

RIGHT GLOVE

With 3¼ mm (UK 10/US 3) needles and Green cast on
42 (50) sts.

* **Next row:** K1, [p1, k1] to last st], p1.

This row sets rib. Work 3 further rows in rib in Green, 2 rows
in Indigo and 10 (12) rows in Red.

Change to 3¾ mm (UK 9/US 5) needles and Yellow and beg
with a k row, work 2 rows in st st. *

SHAPE THUMB

Change to Blue.

Next row: K23 (27), [m1] twice], k19 (23). (44 (52) sts.)

P 1 row.

Change to Green.

Next row: K23 (27), m1, k2, m1, k19 (23). (46 (54) sts.)

P 1 row.

Change to Indigo.

Next row: K23 (27), m1, k4, m1, k19 (23). (48 (56) sts.)

P 1 row.

Next row: K23 (27), m1, k6, m1, k19 (23). (50 (58) sts.)

P 1 row.

Change to Red.

Next row: K23 (27), m1, k8, m1, k19 (23). (52 (60) sts.)

P 1 row.

2nd size only

Next row: K27, m1, k10, m1, k23. (62 sts.)

P 1 row.

Both sizes

DIVIDE FOR THUMB

Change to Yellow.

Next row: K34 (40), turn.

Next row: Cast on and p 1 st, p12 (14), turn.

Next row: Cast on and k 1 st, k to end. (14 (16) sts.)

Beg with a p row, work 15 (17) rows in st st on these
14 (16) sts only.

** SHAPE TOP

Next row: K1, [k2tog] to last st, k1. (8 (9) sts.)

P 1 row.

Next row: K1, [k2tog] to last st (end), k1 (0). (5 (5) sts.)

Break yarn (leaving a long length), thread through rem sts
and draw up tightly. **

*** With RS facing and Yellow, rejoin yarn to rem sts and pick
up and k 2 sts from cast-on sts at base of thumb then k to
end. (42 (50) sts.)

P 1 row in Yellow.

PATTERN

Change to Blue.

Row 1: K 1 row.

Row 2: (using the fairisle method) P3 (2) Blue, p1 Red, [p4
Blue, p1 Red] to last 3 (2) sts], p3 (2) Blue.

Row 3: K2 (1) Blue, k3 Red, [k2 Blue, k3 Red] to last
2 (1) sts], k2 (1) Blue.

Row 4: P2 (1) Blue, p3 Red, [p2 Blue, p3 Red] to last
2 (1) sts], p2 (1) Blue.

Row 5: K3 (2) Blue, k1 Red, [k4 Blue, k1 Red] to last
3 (2) sts], k3 (2) Blue.

Row 6: P 1 row Blue.

Change to Green and beg with a k row, work 2 (4) rows in
st st.

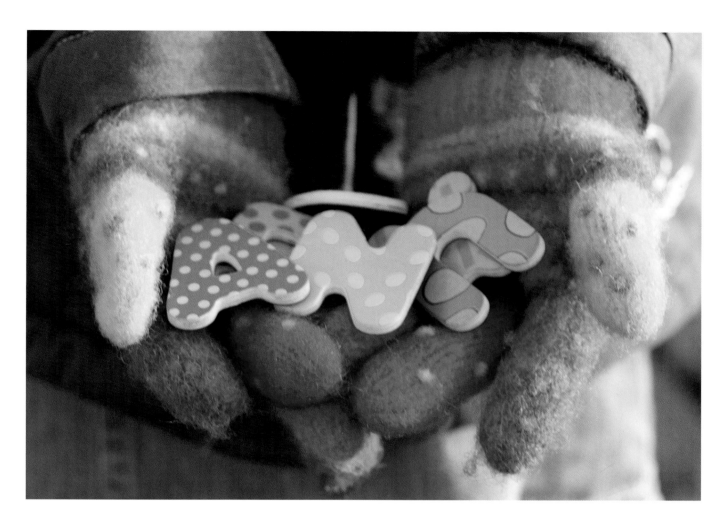

FIRST FINGER

Next row: K27 (32), turn.

Change to Indigo.

Next row: Cast on and p 1 st, p12 (14), turn.

Next row: Cast on and k 1 st, k to end. (14 (16) sts.)

Beg with a p row, work 19 (21) rows in st st on these 14 (16) sts only.

Work as for thumb from ** to **.

SECOND FINGER

With RS facing and Green, rejoin yarn to rem sts and pick up and k 2 sts from cast-on sts at base of first finger then k5 (6), turn.

Change to Red.

Next row: Cast on and p 1 st, p12 (14), turn.

Next row: Cast on and k 1 st, k to end. (14 (16) sts.)

Beg with a p row, work 23 (25) rows in st st on these 14 (16) sts only.

Work as for thumb from ** to **.

THIRD FINGER

With RS facing and Green, rejoin yarn to rem sts and pick up and k 2 sts from cast-on sts at base of second finger then k5 (6), turn.

Change to Blue.

Next row: Cast on and p 1 st, p12 (14), turn.

Next row: Cast on and k 1 st, k to end. (14 (16) sts.)

Beg with a p row, work 19 (21) rows in st st on these 14 (16) sts only.

Work as for thumb from ** to **.

FOURTH FINGER

With RS facing and Green, rejoin yarn to rem sts and pick up and k 2 sts from cast-on sts at base of third finger then k5 (6), turn.

Next row: Cast on and p 1 st, p12 (14).

Next row: Cast on and k 1 st, k to end. (14 (16) sts.) Beg with a p row, work 15 (17) rows in st st on these 14 (16) sts only.

Work as for thumb from ** to **. ***

LEFT GLOVE

With 3¼ mm (UK 10/US 3) needles and Green cast on 42 (50) sts.

Work as for Right Glove from * to *.

SHAPE THUMB

Change to Blue.

Next row: K19 (23), [m1] twice, k23 (27). (44 (52) sts.)

P 1 row.

Change to Green.

Next row: K19 (23), m1, k2, m1, k23 (27). (46 (54) sts.)

P 1 row.

Change to Indigo.

Next row: K19 (23), m1, k4, m1, k23 (27). (48 (56) sts.)

P 1 row.

Next row: K19 (23), m1, k6, m1, k23 (27). (50 (58) sts.)

P 1 row.

Change to Red.

Next row: K19 (23), m1, k8, m1, k23 (27). (52 (60) sts.)

P 1 row.

2nd size only

Next row: K23, m1, k10, m1, k27. (62 sts.)

P 1 row.

Both sizes

DIVIDE FOR THUMB

Change to Yellow.

Next row: K30 (36), turn.

Next row: Cast on and p 1 st, p12 (14), turn.

Next row: Cast on and k 1 st, k to end. (14 (16) sts.) Beg with a p row, work 15 (17) rows in st st on these 14 (16) sts only.

Work as for thumb of Right Glove from ** to **.

Then work as for Right Glove from *** to ***.

FELTING & MAKING UP INSTRUCTIONS

Work in all ends with a needle.

Work French knots in Blue across the Indigo stripe.

Work French knots in Yellow in the centre of each red spot in the pattern section.

Work French knots randomly in Blue on the Yellow thumbs.

Work French knots randomly in Green on the Indigo fingers.

Work French knots randomly in Yellow on the Red fingers.

Work French knots randomly in Indigo on the Blue fingers.

Work French knots randomly in Red on the Green fingers.

Sew all seams using mattress stitch before washing.

Following the instructions on page 14 for machine felting Method A, wash all pieces together to felt.

Reshape whilst damp, dry thoroughly and repeat wash cycle if necessary to achieve desired level of felting.

Flowers in her hair

These pretty flowers are an ideal way of using up oddments of wool yarn for a first felting project. Match colours to favourite outfits and knit whole bouquets for special occasions!

FELTED KNITTING **SKILL LEVEL: EASY**

MEASUREMENTS

One size for ages **2–6 years**

MATERIALS

- 1 x 25 g ball of Jamieson & Smith (Shetland Wool Brokers Ltd) 2 ply Jumper Weight in Purple 20
- Small amounts of Jamieson & Smith (Shetland Wool Brokers Ltd) 2 ply Jumper Weight in Lilac 49, Dark Red/Claret 43, Pink Mixture FC22 and Yellow 91
- Pair of 3¾ mm (UK 9/US 5) knitting needles
- Elastic hair bands, hair clips/slides and Alice band in coordinating colours

ABBREVIATIONS

See page 10

TENSION

Before machine felting:
23 sts and 32 rows to 10 cm (4 in) measured over stocking stitch using 3¾ mm (UK 9/US 5) needles.

FLOWERS

LARGE TUFTED FLOWER

With 3¾ mm (UK 9/US 5) needles and Purple cast on 64 sts.

Beg with a k row, work 4 rows in st st.

Next row: * K4, turn.

Beg with a p row, work 19 rows in st st on these 4 sts only.

Cast off. *

With RS facing, join yarn to rem sts and rep from * to *
14 times more.

With RS facing and Lilac join yarn to rem 4 sts and rep from *
to *.

SMALL TUFTED FLOWERS

With 3¾ mm (UK 9/US 5) needles and Purple cast on 32 sts.

Beg with a k row, work 2 rows in st st.

Next row: ** K2, turn.

Beg with a p row, work 11 rows in st st on these 2 sts only.

Cast off. **

With RS facing, join yarn to rem sts and rep from ** to **
14 times more.

With RS facing and Lilac join yarn to rem 2 sts and rep from
** to **.

LARGE FLOWERS (Make 2)

With 3¾ mm (UK 9/US 5) needles and Purple/Claret make a slip knot and place on needle.

Next row: [Cast on 8 sts (9 sts on needle), cast off 8 sts, sl rem st back onto LH needle] 7 times.

Break yarn thread through rem st and pull tightly. Thread yarn through all sl sts, draw up tightly and fasten off.

SMALL FLOWERS (Make 2)

With 3¾ mm (UK 9/US 5) needles and Lilac/Pink make a slip knot and place on needle.

Next row: [Cast on 5 sts (6 sts on needle), cast off 5 sts, sl rem st back onto LH needle] 7 times.

Break yarn thread through rem st and pull tightly. Thread yarn through all sl sts, draw up tightly and fasten off.

FELTING INSTRUCTIONS

Work in all ends with a needle.

Work French knots in Yellow on the end of the Lilac tuft of the Large Tufted Flower.

Work French knots in contrast colour in centre of Small Flowers.

Following the instructions on page 14 for machine felting Method A, wash all pieces together, placing the items in mesh laundry bags, to felt.

Reshape whilst damp, dry thoroughly and repeat wash cycle if necessary to achieve desired level of felting.

TO MAKE UP

LARGE TUFTED FLOWER

Starting with the Lilac tuft, roll the cast-on edge to form a coil with the Lilac tuft at the centre, sewing through the layers as you go.

Sew the base of the coiled tufts to an elastic hair band.

SMALL TUFTED FLOWERS

Roll in the same way as the Large Tufted Flower and sew each one to an elastic hair band.

FLOWERS

Sew each small flower to the centre of each large flower then sew to hair clips/slides or an Alice band.

Pirate hat

A real favourite with the boys; hours of dressing up fun are guaranteed. Gather ye shipmates and get ready to sail the seven seas for treasures galore!

PLAIN KNITTING

SKILL LEVEL: MODERATE

MEASUREMENTS

Age	2–4	4–6	years
To fit head	51	53	cm
	20	21	in
Actual width	34	36	cm
(point to point)	13½	14	in
Actual length	16	18	cm
	6½	7	in

In the instructions, figures are given for the smaller size first; larger size follows in brackets. Where only one set of figures is given this applies to both sizes.

MATERIALS

- 1 x 50 g ball of Sirdar Click in Black/Black Sheep 138
- 1 x 50 g ball of Sirdar Click in White/Winter White 139
- Pair each of 3¼ mm (UK 10/US 3) and 4 mm (UK 8/US 6) knitting needles

ABBREVIATIONS

See page 10

TENSION

22 sts and 28 rows to 10 cm (4 in) measured over stocking stitch using 4 mm (UK 8/US 6) needles.

HAT

BACK

With 3¼ mm (UK 10/US 3) needles and Black cast on 78 (84) sts.

* Place markers at the 11th and 68th (13th and 72nd sts).

Next row: P0 (1), [k1, p1] to end (last st), k0 (1).

Next row: P1 (0), [k1, p1] to last st (end), k1 (0).

These two rows form moss st. Work 2 further rows in moss st. *

Change to 4 mm (UK 8/US 6) needles and beg with a k row, work 4 (6) rows in st st.

SHAPE SIDES

Dec 1 st at each end of next and foll alt row. (74 (80) sts.)

P 1 row.

Cast off 3 sts at beg of next 2 rows. (68 (74) sts.)

Cast off 3 (4) sts at beg of next 4 rows. (56 (58) sts.)

Work 26 (28) rows dec 1 st at each end of next and every foll alt row. (30 (30) sts.)

2nd size only

Beg with a k row, work 2 rows in st st.

SHAPE TOP

** **Both sizes**

Cast off 3 sts at beg of next 2 rows. (24 sts)

Cast off 4 sts at beg of next 2 rows. (16 sts)
Cast off rem 16 sts. **

FRONT

With 3¼ mm (UK 10/US 3) needles and Black cast on
78 (84) sts.
Work as for Back from * to *.
Change to 4 mm (UK 8/US 6) needles and beg with a k row,
work 2 (4) rows in st st.

PLACE CHART

Next row: K32 (35), k across 1st row of chart using the
intarsia method, k to end.
Next row: P31 (34), p across 2nd row of chart, p to end.
Using the intarsia method, cont to work the rem 26 rows of
the chart as set, **at the same time** shape as folls.

SHAPE SIDES

Dec 1 st at each end of next and foll alt row. (74 (80) sts.)
P 1 row.
Cast off 3 sts at beg of next 2 rows. (68 (74) sts.)
Cast off 3 (4) sts at beg of next 4 rows. (56 (58) sts.)

Cont to work the rem 16 rows of the chart as set, **at the
same time** cont to shape as folls.
Work 26 (28) rows dec 1 st at each end of next and every foll
alt row. (30 (30) sts.)
2nd size only
Beg with a k row, work 2 rows in st st.

SHAPE TOP

Work as for Back from ** to **.

TO MAKE UP

Sew in all ends.
With right sides together, sew front and back sections
together using backstitch following the line of the shapings.
Then sew the cast-on edges together from the markers to
the side seams.

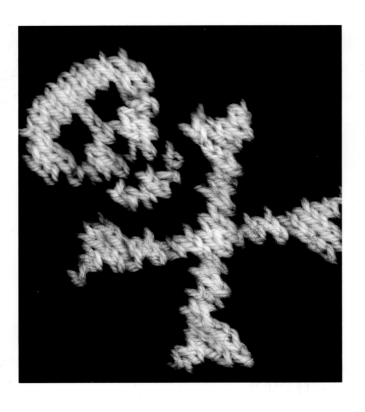

KEY

☐   Black

×   White

Corsages

These are sure to be coveted by mothers and daughters alike and add a finishing touch to any outfit. Use up any scraps of wool you have to create endless variations to clip to bags, knitwear and coats.

FELTED KNITTING **SKILL LEVEL: MODERATE** ★★☆

MEASUREMENTS
One size   for ages **2–6 years**

MATERIALS
- 1 x 25 g ball of Jamieson & Smith (Shetland Wool Brokers Ltd) 2 ply Jumper Weight in Bright Red 93
- Small amounts of Jamieson & Smith (Shetland Wool Brokers Ltd) 2 ply Jumper Weight in Orange 125, Light Orange Mixture FC7 and Turquoise/Seafoam 75
- Pair each of 3¾ mm (UK 9/US 5) double pointed and 3¾ mm (UK 9/US 5) knitting needles
- Brooch pins
- Buttons and beads if required

ABBREVIATIONS
See page 10

TENSION
Before machine felting:
23 sts and 32 rows to 10 cm (4 in) measured over stocking stitch using 3¾ mm (UK 9/US 5) needles.

CORSAGES

PETALS (Make 6)
With 3¾ mm (UK 9/US 5) needles and Bright Red cast on 5 sts.
Beg with a k row, work 2 rows in st st.
Next row: Inc in 1st st, k to last st, m1, k1.
P 1 row.
Rep the last 2 rows once more. (9 sts.)
Beg with a k row, work 4 rows in st st.
Next row: K1, skpo, k to last 2 sts, k2tog.
P1 row.

Rep the last 2 rows once more. (5 sts.)
Cast off.

LARGE FLOWER
With 3¾ mm (UK 9/US 5) needles and Orange cast on 9 sts.
Next row: Inc in every st. (18 sts.)
P 1 row.
Next row: * K3, turn.
P1 row.
Next row: Inc in 1st st, k to last st, m1, k1.
P1 row.
Rep the last 2 rows once more. (7 sts.)
Beg with a k row, work 2 rows in st st.

Next row: K1, skpo, k to last 2 sts, k2tog.

P1 row.

Rep the last 2 rows once more. (3 sts.)

Cast off. *

With RS facing join yarn to rem sts and rep from * to *

5 times more.

MEDIUM FLOWER

With 3¾ mm (UK 9/US 5) needles and Light Orange Mixture
cast on 68 sts.

P 1 row.

Next row: K2, [k1, sl this st back onto LH needle, pass the
next 8 sts over the top of this st and off the needle, [yrn]
twice], k the sl st again, k2] to end.

Next row: P1, [p2tog, p1, p1 tbl, p1], to last st, p1.

Next row: [K2tog] to end. (13 sts.)

P1 row.

Next row: K1, [k2tog] to end]. (7 sts.)

Break yarn, thread through rem sts, pull up tightly and
fasten off.

SMALL FLOWER

With 3¾ mm (UK 9/US 5) needles and Bright Red cast on
35sts.

Next row: [K1, cast off 5 sts (2 sts on RH needle)] to end.
(10 sts.)

Next row: [P2tog] to end. (5 sts.)

Break yarn, thread through rem sts, pull up tightly and
fasten off.

CORD

With 3¾ mm (UK 9/US 5) double pointed needles and
Seafoam cast on 4 sts.

K 1 row.

Next row: ** Without turning the work, and RS facing, slide
the sts to the other end of the needle and, pulling the yarn
from the left hand side of the sts to the right across the
back, k1 tbl, k3. **

Rep from ** to **, remembering to pull the yarn tightly across
the back and always working a k row, until the cord meas
20 cm (8 in).

Cast off.

FELTING INSTRUCTIONS

Work in all ends with a needle and join edges of flowers
together to form flower shapes.

Make 2 small pom poms in Bright Red.

Following the instructions on page 14 for machine felting
Method A, wash all pieces together, placing the items in
mesh laundry bags, to felt.

Reshape whilst damp, dry thoroughly and repeat wash cycle
if necessary to achieve desired level of felting.

TO MAKE UP

Sew Petals in between and behind each petal of the Large
Flower.

Sew the Medium Flower to the centre of the Large Flower
and the Small Flower to the centre of the Medium Flower.

Fold the cord in half and sew the centre point to the reverse
of the Corsage. Sew a pom pom to each end of the cord.

Sew a brooch pin to the reverse of the Corsage.

Make other Corsages from Medium Flowers decorated with
beaded, felted pom poms or buttons at the centres.

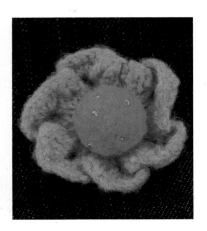

Softie slippers

These slippers are knitted from a yarn that felts beautifully, resulting in lovely soft footwear that's as comfy as a pair of socks. The large felted pom poms add a cute touch and non slip soles make them safe.

FELTED KNITTING **SKILL LEVEL: MODERATE**

MEASUREMENTS

Age	2–3	3–4	4–5	5–6	years
To fit shoe size (approximately)	4–6	6–8	8–10	10–12	
Actual length	16	17.5	19	21	cm
	6¼	7	7½	8¼	in

In the instructions, figures are given for the smallest size first; larger sizes follow in brackets. Where only one set of figures is given this applies to all sizes.

MATERIALS

- 1 (1:1:2) x 50 g balls of Rowan Scottish Tweed DK in Purple/Thistle 016
- 1 (1:1:2) x 50 g balls of Rowan Scottish Tweed DK in Lilac/Lavender 005
- 1 x 50 g ball of Rowan Scottish Tweed DK in Pink/Brilliant Pink 010
- Pair of 6 mm (UK 4/US 10) knitting needles
- 3.5 mm (UK 9/US E/4) crochet hook
- Rubberised, textured, non-slip matting – the kind used to line trays

ABBREVIATIONS

See page 10

TENSION

Before machine felting:

14½ sts and 20 rows to 10 cm (4 in) measured over stocking stitch using 6 mm (UK 4/US 10) needles.

After machine felting (Method A):

16 sts and 26 rows to 10 cm (4 in) measured over stocking stitch.

SLIPPER

SOLE (Make 4)

With 6 mm (UK 4/US 10) needles and Purple cast on 4 sts.
Beg with a k row, work 2 rows in st st.

SHAPE HEEL

Next row: Inc 1 st (1 st:2 sts:2 sts) at each end of row.
P 1 row.
Next row: Inc 1 st at each end of row. (8 (8:10:10) sts.)
P 1 row.
Beg with a k row, work 28 (32:36:40) rows in st st inc 1 st at each end of 8th & 16th (10th & 20th:12th & 24th:14th & 28th) rows. (12 (12:14:14) sts.)

SHAPE TOE

Next row: K1, skpo, k6 (6:8:8), k2tog, k1.
(10 (10:12:12) sts.)
P 1 row.
Next row: K1, skpo, k4 (4:6:6), k2tog, k1. (8 (8:10:10) sts.)
P 1 row.
Next row: K1, skpo, k2 (2:4:4), k2tog, k1. (6 (6:8:8) sts.)
P 1 row.
Next row: K1, skpo, k0 (0:2:2), k2tog, k1. (4 (4:6:6) sts.)
P 1 row.
Cast off rem 4 (4:6:6) sts.

UPPER (Make 2)

With 6 mm (UK 4/US 10) needles and Lilac cast on
64 (70:76:82) sts.
Beg with a k row, work 4 rows in st st.

SHAPE TOE

Next row: K24 (27:30:33), [skpo] twice, k8, [k2tog] twice, turn.
Next row: P12, turn.
Next row: [Skpo] twice, k4, [k2tog] twice, turn.
Next row: P to end.
Next row: K23 (26:29:32), skpo, k6, k2tog, K23 (26:29:32).
(54 (60:66:72) sts.)

P 1 row.

Next row: K23 (26:29:32), skpo, k4, k2tog, K23 (26:29:32). (52 (58:64:70) sts.)

P 1 row.

Next row: K23 (26:29:32), skpo, k2, k2tog, K23 (26:29:32). (50 (56:62:68) sts.)

P 1 row.

1st size only

Change to Pink.

Next row: K23, skpo, k2tog, K23. (48 sts.)

P 1 row.

Cast off.

2nd, 3rd and 4th sizes

Next row: K (26:29:32), skpo, k2tog, K (26:29:32). (54:60:66) sts.)

P 1 row.

2nd size only

Change to Pink.

Next row: K (25), skpo, k2tog, K (25). (52 sts.)

P 1 row.

Cast off.

3rd and 4th sizes

Next row: K (28:31), skpo, k2tog, K (28:31). (58:64 sts.)

P 1 row.

3rd size only

Change to Pink.

Next row: K (27), skpo, k2tog, K (27). (56 sts.)

P 1 row.

Cast off.

4th size

Change to Pink.

Next row: K (30), skpo, k2tog, K (30). (62 sts)

P 1 row.

Next row: K (29), skpo, k2tog, K (29). (60 sts)

P 1 row.

Cast off.

FELTING INSTRUCTIONS

Work in all ends with a needle.

Make 2 pom poms in Pink approximately 5 cm (2 in) in diameter.

Following the instructions on page 14 for machine felting Method A, wash all pieces together, placing the pom poms in a mesh laundry bag, to felt.

Reshape whilst damp, dry thoroughly and repeat wash cycle if necessary to achieve desired level of felting.

TO MAKE UP

With wrong sides together, oversew each pair of soles together all around edges.

With right sides together sew centre back seam of each upper.

Place lower edge of upper against the oversewn edge of the soles and, using Lilac yarn, sew all around to join upper to sole.

Sew pom poms to centre fronts of each upper.

With a 3.5 mm (UK 9/US E/4) crochet hook and Pink, make two 55 cm (21½ in) lengths of chain Thread through top edge of each upper, draw up to fit foot and tie in a bow at front.

Cut a piece of non slip matting for each toe and heel section of sole and sew to each slipper to prevent slipping when wearing.

Dinosaur duffle

A hardwearing but fun bag just the right size for those essential items needed for an afternoon exploring and discovering. The cute motif and lovely colours will appeal to both boys and girls.

FELTED
KNITTING

SKILL LEVEL:
MODERATE

MEASUREMENTS

One size   for ages **2–6 years**
Bag   Approximately 25 cm (10 in) wide,
                     30 cm (12 in) long

MATERIALS

• 3 x 50 g balls of Twilleys of Stamford Freedom Wool in Green/Pale Green 411
• 1 x 50 g ball of Twilleys of Stamford Freedom Wool in Khaki/Olive Green 420
• 1 x 50 g ball of Twilleys of Stamford Freedom Spirit in Multi/Essence 507
• Pair each of 5 mm (UK 6/US 8) double pointed, 5 mm (UK 6/US 8) and 10 mm (UK 000/US 15) knitting needles
• Stranded embroidery thread in Black and White

ABBREVIATIONS

See page 10

TENSION

Freedom Wool
Before machine felting:
10 sts and 12 rows to 10 cm (4 in) measured over stocking stitch using 10 mm (UK 000/US 15) needles.
After machine felting (Method B):
10 sts and 16 rows to 10 cm (4 in) measured over stocking stitch.
Freedom Spirit
18 sts and 28 rows to 10 cm (4 in) measured over moss stitch using 5 mm (UK 6/US 8) needles, before machine felting.

BAG

BACK

* With 10 mm (UK 000/US 15) needles and Green cast on 26 sts.

Beg with a k row, work 2 rows in st st.

MAKE BOTTOM EYELETS

Next row: K2, yfwd, k2tog, k19, yfwd, k2tog, k1. *

Beg with a p row, work 43 rows in st st.

** **Make top eyelets**

Next row: K3, [yfwd, k2tog, k2] twice, yfwd, k2tog, k1, [yfwd, k2tog, k2] 3 times.

P 1 row.

Cast off. **

FRONT

Work as for back from * to *.

Beg with a p row, work 11 rows in st st.

PLACE DINOSAUR

Next row: K1, k across 24 sts of first row of chart using the intarsia method, k1.

Please note: 2 strands of Multi are used together in this section.

Work the rem 17 rows of the chart as set.

Next row: Beg with a k row, work 14 rows in st st.

Work as for back from ** to **.

SPIKE TRIM

With 5 mm (UK 6/US 8) needles and Multi cast on 150 sts.

Next row: K1, [p1, k1] to last st, p1

Next row: P1, [k1, p1] to last st, k1.

These 2 rows form moss st. Cont in moss st throughout.

Row 3: *** Work 10, turn.

Work on these 10 sts only as folls:

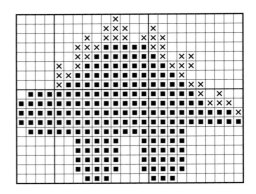

KEY

☐   Green

■   Khaki

×   Multi (2 strand)

Work 3 rows in moss st.

Row 7: P2tog, work 6, k2tog.

Next and every foll alt row: Work 1 row.

Row 9: K2tog, work 4, p2tog.

Row 11: P2tog, work 2, k2tog.

Row 13: K2tog, p2tog.

Row 14: K2tog, break yarn and thread through rem st. ***

With RS facing, rejoin yarn to rem sts and rep from *** to *** 14 times more.

CORD STRAP (Make 2)

With 5 mm (UK 6/US 8) double pointed needles and Multi, cast on 3 sts.

K 1 row.

Next row: **** Without turning the work, and RS facing, slide the sts to the other end of the needle and, pulling the yarn from the left hand side of the sts to the right across the back, k1 tbl, k2. ****

Rep from **** to ****, remembering to pull the yarn tightly across the back and always working a k row, until the cord meas 150 cm (59 in).

Cast off.

FELTING INSTRUCTIONS

Work in all ends with a needle.

Following the instructions on page 15 for machine felting Method B, wash all pieces together, placing the cord and spike trim in mesh laundry bags, to felt.

Reshape whilst damp and dry thoroughly.

TO MAKE UP

Embroider eye on dinosaur using black embroidery thread and satin stitch. Work a small highlight in eye with white thread. Embroider mouth using black embroidery thread and stem stitch.

Lay the back piece of the bag face down on a flat surface. Then lay the spike trim, beginning just below the top eyelets, down the right hand side, along the bottom and up the left hand side so that the points point outwards and the straight edge lays just on the edge of the bag back piece.

Lay the front bag piece on top, matching up top and bottom eyelets. Stitch through all thicknesses using sewing thread, keeping close to the edge and curving the bottom corners slightly.

Take one of the cords and thread it in and out of the eyelets at the top of the front, around the side and through the eyelets in the back piece. Repeat with the other cord in the opposite direction. Pull each of the cords until they are of equal length. You should have a set of two cords on either side of the bag. Pass the front cord from each side through from the front to the back of the bottom eyelets and sew the ends of each cord together.

Bunny bucket

Just the right size for keeping small toys and treasures in; this little bunny, with his cute face and ears, would look lovely sitting on a nursery shelf or taken on days out.

FELTED KNITTING

SKILL LEVEL: **EASY**

MEASUREMENTS

One size — for ages **2–6 years**

Bag — Approximately 15 cm (6 in) high

MATERIALS

- 2 x 50 g balls of Twilleys of Stamford Freedom Wool in Pale Blue 418
- Pair of 10 mm (UK 000/US 15) knitting needles
- Stranded embroidery thread in Black and White
- Felt fabric for lining 60 x 25 cm (23½ x 10 in)
- Cardboard

ABBREVIATIONS

See page 10

TENSION

Before machine felting:

10 sts and 12 rows to 10 cm (4 in) measured over stocking stitch using 10 mm (UK 000/US 15) needles.

After machine felting (Method B):

10 sts and 16 rows to 10 cm (4 in) measured over stocking stitch.

BUCKET

BASE

With 10 mm (UK 000/US 15) needles and Pale Blue cast on 2 sts.

Working in st st throughout, cont as follows

K 1 row.

Cast on 2 sts at beg of next 2 rows. (6 sts.)

P 1 row.

Inc 1 st at each end of next 3 rows. (12 sts.)

Beg with a p row, work 6 rows in st st.

Dec 1 st at each end of next 3 rows. (6 sts.)

K 1 row.

Cast off 2 sts at beg of next 2 rows. (2 sts.)

P 1 row.

Cast off.

SIDE

With 10 mm (UK 000/US 15) needles and Pale Blue cast on 38 sts.

Beg with a k row, work 6 rows in st st.

Next row: K9, m1, k20, m1, k9. (40 sts.)

Beg with a p row, work 9 rows in st st.

Next row: K5, m1, [k10, m1] 3 times, k5. (44 sts.)

Beg with a p row, work 7 rows in st st.

Shape ears

Next row: Cast off 18 sts, k1, turn.

* Work on these 2 sts only as follows.
Beg with a p row, work 5 rows in st st.
Next row: Inc 1 st at each end of row. (4 sts.)
Beg with a p row, work 3 rows in st st.
Next row: Skpo, k2tog. (2 sts.)
P 1 row.
Next row: K2tog, break yarn and thread through rem st. *
With RS facing, rejoin yarn to rem sts and cont as follows.
Cast off 4 sts, k1, turn.
Work as for 1st ear from * to *.
With RS facing, rejoin yarn to rem sts and cast off.

HANDLE

With 10 mm (UK 000/US 15) needles and Pale Blue cast on 32 sts.
Beg with a k row, work 8 rows in st st.
Cast off.

FELTING INSTRUCTIONS

Work in all ends with a needle.
Following the instructions on page 15 for machine felting Method B, wash all pieces together to felt.
Reshape whilst damp and dry thoroughly.

TO MAKE UP

Use the side and base pieces as patterns to cut the same pieces from felt fabric for the lining.
Sew the centre back seam of the knitted side piece. Sew the base to the bottom of the tube just formed.
Repeat with the felt fabric lining pieces.
Roll the two long edges of the handle towards each other and join.
Sew inside the bucket sides just below the top edge.
Embroider eyes and nose in black embroidery thread using satin stitch and stem stitch respectively. Sew a small white highlight in each eye.
Cut a circle of cardboard to fit inside the bucket base.
Place the felt lining inside the bucket with wrong sides together, and sew the lining to the knitted pieces along the top edge and around the ears.

Elliot's hoody

A smooth, stripy, cotton knit that's perfect for your boy to throw on over a t-shirt, and head out for a summer evening game of football. A favourite with my son as it's so comfy to wear.

PLAIN KNITTING

SKILL LEVEL: MODERATE

MEASUREMENTS

Age	2–3	3–4	4–5	5–6	years
To fit chest	56	58	61	63	cm
	22	23	24	25	in
Actual width	61	66	72	79	cm
	24	26	28½	31	in
Actual length	36	39.5	42	45.5	cm
	14	15½	16½	18	in

In the instructions, figures are given for the smallest size first; larger sizes follow in brackets. Where only one set of figures is given this applies to all sizes.

MATERIALS

- 3 (3:4:4) x 50 g balls of Sirdar Luxury Soft Cotton DK in Navy/French Navy 654
- 2 (2:3:3) x 50 g balls of Sirdar Luxury Soft Cotton DK in Green/Sage 657
- Pair each of 3¾ mm (UK 9/US 5) and 4 mm (UK 8/US 6) knitting needles

ABBREVIATIONS

See page 10

TENSION

22 sts and 28 rows to 10 cm (4 in) measured over stocking stitch using 4 mm (UK 8/US 6) needles

front and back

HOODY

BACK

With 3¾ mm (UK 9/US 5) needles and Navy cast on
67 (73:79:87) sts.
Row 1: P0 (2:0:0), k2 (3:2:0), [p3, k3] to last 5 (2:5:3) sts,
p3 (2:3:3), k2 (0:2:0).
Row 2: K0 (2:0:0), p2 (3:2:0), [k3, p3] to last 5 (2:5:3) sts,
k3 (2:3:3), p2 (0:2:0).
Rep the last 2 rows 4 (5:5:6) times more.
Change to 4 mm (UK 8/US 6) needles and Green.
Beg with a k row and working st st stripes of 20 rows
Green, 20 rows Navy throughout work until back meas
22 (24.5:26:28.5) cm (8½ (9½:10:11) in) ending with a
WS row.

SHAPE ARMHOLES

Cast off 3 (4:4:4) sts at beg of next 2 rows.
(61 (65:71:79) sts.)
Dec 1 st at each end of next 3 (3:3:5) rows.
(55 (59:65:69) sts.)
Dec 1 st at each end of every foll alt row until 53 (55:61:65)
sts rem.
Cont in st st and stripe sequence as set until armhole meas
14 (15:16:17) cm (5½ (6:6½:7) in) ending with a WS row.

SHAPE SHOULDERS AND NECK

Cast off 4 (5:5:6) sts at beg of next 2 rows.
(45 (45:51:53) sts.)
Next row: Cast off 4 (5:5:6) sts, k8 (7:9:8), turn.
Work on these 9 (8:10:9) sts only as folls.
Next row: Cast off 4 sts, p to end.
Cast off rem 5 (4:6:5) sts.
With RS facing, rejoin yarn to rem sts and cont as folls.
Cast off centre 19 (19:21:23) sts, k to end.
Next row: Cast off 4 (5:5:6) sts, p to end.
Next row: Cast off 4 sts, k to end.
Cast off rem 5 (4:6:5) sts.

FRONT

Work as for back until 12 (14:14:16) rows less have been
worked than on back to start of shoulder shaping, ending
with a WS row.

SHAPE NECK

Next row: K19 (21:23:25), turn.
Work on these 19 (21:23:25) sts only as follows.
Dec 1 st at neck edge on next 4 rows. (15 (17:19:21) sts.)
Dec 1 st at neck edge on every foll alt row until 13 (14:16:17)
sts rem.
Work 3 rows.

SHAPE SHOULDER

Cast off 4 (5:5:6) sts at beg of next and foll alt row.
Work 1 row.
Cast off rem 5 (4:6:5) sts.
With RS facing, rejoin yarn to rem sts and cont as folls.
Cast off centre 15 (13:15:15) sts, k to end.
Dec 1 st at neck edge on next 4 rows. (15 (17:19:21) sts.)
Dec 1 st at neck edge on every foll alt row until
13 (14:16:17) sts rem.
Work 2 rows.

SHAPE SHOULDER

Cast off 4 (5:5:6) sts at beg of next and foll alt row.
Work 1 row.
Cast off rem 5 (4:6:5) sts.

LEFT HOOD

With 4 mm (UK 8/US 6) needles and Navy cast on 7 sts.
Row 1 (RS): K2, [p1, k1] twice, p1.
Row 2: [P1, k1] twice, p3.
These 2 rows set moss st edge. Keeping 5 sts at front edge
in moss st throughout and working stripes of 20 rows Navy,
20 rows Green throughout, cont as folls.
Cast on 6 sts at beg of next and foll alt row, 4 (5:5:6) sts at
beg of foll 3 alt rows, and 4 sts at beg of foll alt row.
(35 (38:38:41) sts.)
Work 5 rows, ending with a WS row.

Inc 1 st at beg of next and every foll 6th row to
41 (44:44:47) sts.
Cont straight until hood meas 24.5 (26:26:28) cm
(9½ (10:10:11) in) along moss st edge, ending with a WS row.
Dec 1 st at beg of next and foll 4th row. (39 (42:42:45) sts.)
Work 3 rows.
Dec 1 st at shaped edge on next 3 rows. (36 (39:39:42) sts.)
Next row (WS): Cast off 4 sts, work to last 2 sts, p2tog.
Next row (RS): Dec 1 st at beg of row, work to end.
Next row (WS): Cast off 4 sts, p to last 2 sts, p2tog.
Cast off rem 25 (28:28:31) sts.

RIGHT HOOD

With 4 mm (UK 8/US 6) needles and Navy cast on 7 sts.
Row 1 (RS): [P1, k1] twice, p1, k2.
Row 2: Cast on and p 6 sts, p3, [k1, p1] twice.
These 2 rows set moss st edge. Keeping 5 sts at front edge
in moss st throughout and working stripes of 20 rows Navy,
20 rows Green throughout, cont as folls.
Work 1 row.
Cast on 6 sts at beg of next row, 4 (5:5:6) sts at beg of foll
3 alt rows, and 4 sts at beg of foll alt row. (35 (38:38:41) sts.)
Work 5 rows, ending with a RS row.
Inc 1 st at beg of next and every foll 6th row to
41 (44:44:47) sts.
Cont straight until hood meas 24.5 (26:26:28) cm
(9½ (10:10:11) in) along moss st edge, ending with a RS row.
Dec 1 st at end of next and foll 4th row. (39 (42:42:45) sts.)
Work 3 rows.
Dec 1 st at shaped edge on next 2 rows. (37 (40:40:43) sts.)
Next row (RS): Cast off 4 sts at beg and dec 1 st at end
of row.
Next row (WS): Dec 1 st at beg of row, work to end.
Rep last 2 rows once more.
Cast off rem 25 (28:28:31) sts.

POCKET

With 4 mm (UK 8/US 6) needles and Green cast on
48 (52:56:60) sts.

Beg with a k row, work 10 rows in st st.

Change to Navy, and beg with a k row, work 2 (4:4:6) rows
in st st.

Cast off 3 sts at beg of next 4 rows. (36 (40:44:48) sts.)

Dec 1 st at each end of next and every foll alt row until
30 (34:36:40) sts rem.

Beg with a p row, work 9 (7:5:3) rows in st st.

Change to Green, and beg with a k row, work
4 (10:10:14) rows in st st.

Cast off.

POCKET EDGINGS

With RS facing, 3¾ mm (UK 9/US 5) needles and Navy, pick
up and knit 13 (17:17:19) sts around shaped pocket edge.

Row 1 (WS): P2 (0:0:0), k3 (1:1:2), [p3, k3] to last
2 (4:4:5) sts], p2 (3:3:3), k0 (1:1:2).

Row 2 (RS): K2 (0:0:0), p3 (1:1:2), [k3, p3] to last
2 (4:4:5) sts], k2 (3:3:3), p0 (1:1:2).

Rep row 1 once more, ending with a WS row.

Cast off evenly in rib.

Join shoulder seams using backstitch.

ARMHOLE EDGINGS

With RS facing, 3¾ mm (UK 9/US 5) needles and Navy, pick
up and knit 66 (72:78:84) sts around armhole edge.

Row 1 (WS): [K3, p3] to end.

Rep last row 3 times more, ending with a RS row.

Cast off evenly in rib.

TO MAKE UP

Place pocket centrally on front, matching stripes. Sew
bottom, top and side edges to front using swiss darning
stitches to hide the edges of the pocket and make an
invisible join.

Sew front to back at side seams.

Sew centre back and top seam of hood.

Place centre back seam of hood to centre point of back
neck and front edges of hood to centre point of front neck,
pin lower edge of hood to neck edge and sew in place.

Flowers and lace cardigan

Fresh colours, flowers and lace combine to make a very pretty cardigan to wear over sundresses on summer evenings. Using a bamboo yarn that has a lovely drape and softness, this will be adored by any little girl.

PLAIN KNITTING

SKILL LEVEL: ADVANCED ★ ★ ★

MEASUREMENTS

Age	2–3	3–4	4–5	5–6	years
To fit chest	56	58	61	63	cm
	22	23	24	25	in
Actual width	59	64	70	73	cm
	23	25	27½	29	in
Actual length	34	36	39	43	cm
	13½	14	15½	17	in
Sleeve length	24	26.5	29.5	33	cm
	9½	10½	11½	13	in

In the instructions, figures are given for the smallest size first; larger sizes follow in brackets. Where only one set of figures is given this applies to all sizes.

MATERIALS

- 4 (5: 6: 7) x 50 g balls of Sirdar Snuggly Baby Bamboo in Pale Blue/Waterbaby 138
- 1 (1: 1: 2) x 50 g balls of Sirdar Snuggly Baby Bamboo in Lilac/Little Lilac 137
- 1 (1: 1: 2) x 50 g balls of Sirdar Snuggly Baby Bamboo in Mauve/Tulip 136
- 1 x 50 g ball of Sirdar Snuggly Baby Bamboo in Pale Green/Willow 133
- Pair each of 3¼ mm (UK 10/US 3) and 4 mm (UK 8/US 6) knitting needles

ABBREVIATIONS

See page 10

TENSION

22 sts and 28 rows to 10 cm (4 in) measured over stocking stitch using 4 mm (UK 8/US 6) needles.

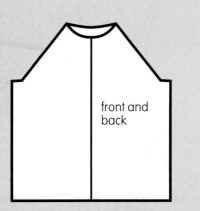

front and back

sleeve

CARDIGAN

BACK

With 3¼ mm (UK 10/US 3) needles and Waterbaby cast on 67 (73:79:83) sts.

*Beg with a k row, work 4 rows in st st.

Change to 4 mm (UK 8/US 6) needles and, beg with a k row, work 4 rows in st st.*

PLACE CHART

Using the intarsia technique, work across the first row of the corresponding size from Chart A.

Work the rem 17 rows of the chart in st st.

Beg with a k row, work 4 rows in st st.

LACE EYELET PATTERN

Next row: K5 (8:11:2), yfwd, k2tog, [k9, yfwd, k2tog] to last 5 (8:11:2) sts, k5 (8:11: 2).

Beg with a p row, work 7 rows in st st.

Next row: K10 (2:5:7), yfwd, k2tog, [k9, yfwd, k2tog] to last 11 (3:6:8) sts, k11 (3:6: 8).

Beg with a p row, work 7 rows in st st.

These 16 rows form lace patt. Cont in patt as set until Back meas 22 (23.5:26:28.5) cm (8½ (9: 10:11) in) from cast-on edge, ending with a WS row.

SHAPE RAGLANS

Cont in lace patt as set throughout, cont as follows.

Cast off 4 (4:4:5) sts at beg of next 2 rows.

(59 (65:71:73) sts.)

Work 8 (8:12:8) rows dec 1 st at each end of every row.

(43 (49:47:57) sts.)

KEY

☐   Waterbaby

▲   Tulip

ᴗ   Little Lilac

-   Willow

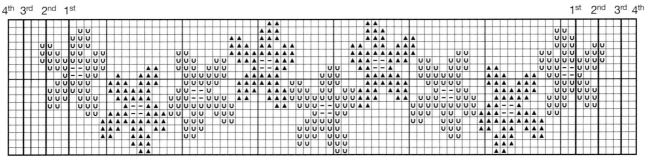

CHART A

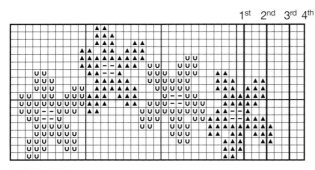

CHART B

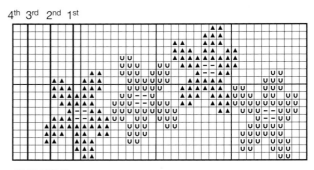

CHART C

Work 22 (24:22:30) rows dec 1 st at each end of next and every foll alt row. (21 (25:25:27) sts.)
Leave rem 21 (25:25:27) sts on a holder.

LEFT FRONT

With 3¼ mm (UK 10/US 3) needles and Waterbaby cast on 31 (34:37:39) sts.
Work as Back from * to *.

PLACE CHART

Using the intarsia technique, work across the first row of the corresponding size from Chart B.
Work the rem 17 rows of the chart in st st.
Beg with a k row, work 4 rows in st st.

LACE EYELET PATTERN

Next row: K5 (8:11:2), yfwd, k2tog, [k9, yfwd, k2tog] to last 2 sts, k2.
Beg with a p row, work 7 rows in st st.
Next row: K10 (2:5:7), yfwd, k2tog, [k9, yfwd, k2tog] to last 8 sts, k8.

Beg with a p row, work 7 rows in st st.
These 16 rows form lace patt. Cont in patt as set until Left Front meas 22 (23.5:26:28.5) cm (8½ (9:10:11) in) from cast-on edge, ending with a WS row.

SHAPE RAGLAN

Cont in lace patt as set throughout, cont as follows.
Cast off 4 (4:4:5) sts, k to end. (27 (30:33:34) sts.)
P 1 row.
Work 8 (8:12:8) rows dec 1 st at raglan edge on every row. (19 (22:21:26) sts.)
Work 15 (17:17:19) rows dec 1 st at raglan edge on next and every foll alt row. (11 (13:12:16) sts.)

SHAPE NECK

Next row: Cast off 2 (5:5:5) sts, p to end. (9 (8:7:11) sts.)
1st & 3rd sizes only
Work 4 (3) rows dec 1 st at raglan edge on next and foll alt row, **at the same time**, dec 1 st at neck edge on every row. (3 (2) sts.)
Work 1 (0) row dec 1 (0) st at raglan edge only. (2 (2) sts.)
2nd & 4th sizes only
Work (5:8) rows dec 1 st at each end of next and every foll alt row. ((2:3) sts.)
4th size only
Work 1 row dec 1 st at raglan edge only. (2 sts.)
All sizes
Next row: P2tog, break yarn, thread through rem st and fasten off.

RIGHT FRONT

With 3¼ mm (UK 10/US 3) needles and Waterbaby cast on 31 (34:37:39) sts.
Work as for Back from * to *.

PLACE CHART

Using the intarsia technique, work across the first row of the corresponding size from Chart C.
Work the rem 17 rows of the chart in st st.
Beg with a k row, work 4 rows in st st.

LACE EYELET PATTERN

Next row: K2, yon, k2tog, [k9, yfwd, k2tog] to last
5 (8:11:2) sts, k 5 (8:11:2).

Beg with a p row, work 7 rows in st st.

Next row: K8, yfwd, k2tog, [k9, yfwd, k2tog] to last
10 (2:5:7) sts, k10 (2:5:7).

Beg with a p row, work 7 rows in st st.

These 16 rows form lace patt. Cont in patt as set until Right
Front meas 22 (23.5:26:28.5) cm (8½ (9:10:11) in) from
cast-on edge, ending with a RS row.

SHAPE RAGLAN

Cont in lace patt as set throughout, cont as follows.

Cast off 4 (4:4:5) sts, p to end. (27 (30:33:34) sts.)

Work 8 (8:12:8) rows dec 1 st at raglan edge on every row.
(19 (22:21:26) sts.)

Work 14 (16:16:18) rows dec 1 st at raglan edge on next
and every foll alt row. (12 (14:13:17) sts.)

SHAPE NECK

Next row: Cast off 2 (5:5:5) sts, k to last 2 sts, k2tog.
(9 (8:7:11) sts.)

P 1 row.

1st & 3rd sizes only

Work 4 (3) rows dec 1 st at neck edge on every row, **at the
same time**, dec 1 st at raglan edge on next and foll alt row.
(3 (2) sts.)

Work 1 (0) row dec 1 (0) st at raglan edge only. (2 (2) sts.)

2nd & 4th sizes only

Work (5:8) rows dec 1 st at each end of next and every foll

alt row. ((2:3) sts.)

4th size only

Work 1 row dec 1 st at raglan edge only. (2 sts.)

All sizes

Next row: P2tog, break yarn, thread through rem st and
fasten off.

SLEEVE (Make 2)

With 3¼ mm (UK 10/US 3) needles and Waterbaby cast on
33 (37:39:41) sts.

Work as for Back from * to *.

PLACE CHART

Using the intarsia technique, work across the first row of the
corresponding size from Chart D, **at the same time**, inc 1
st at each end of 2nd and every foll 6th row to 47 (49:51:65).
Work the rem 17 rows of the chart in st st incorporating the
new sts into the patt as shown on the chart.

Beg with a k row, work 4 rows in st st cont to inc as set.

LACE EYELET PATTERN

Cont to inc as set and cont as follows.

Next row: K9 (11:12:2), yfwd, k2tog, [k9, yfwd, k2tog] to
last 8 (10:11:1) sts, k8 (10:11:1).

Beg with a p row, work 7 rows in st st cont to inc as set.

Next row: Inc in first st k3 (5:6:7), yfd, k2tog, [k9, yfwd,
k2tog] to last 4 (6:7:8) sts, k3 (5:6:7), inc last st.

Beg with a p row, work 7 rows in st st cont to inc as set.

These 16 rows form lace patt. Cont in patt, inc as set and
keeping the eyelets on the same sts throughout as set and

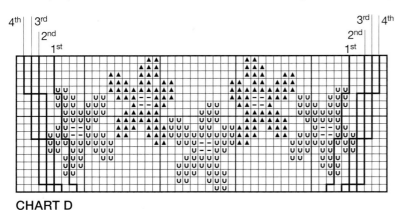

CHART D

KEY

☐ Waterbaby

▲ Tulip

ᴜ Little Lilac

− Willow

incorporating new sts into the pattern, until there are
51 (57:61:69) sts.
Cont without shaping until sleeve meas
24 (26.5:29.5:33) cm (9½ (10½:11½:13) in) from cast-on
edge, ending with a WS row.

SHAPE RAGLAN

Cont in lace patt as set throughout, cont as follows.
Cast off 4 (4:4:5) sts at beg of next 2 rows.
(43 (49:53:59) sts.)
Work 2 (4:2:4) rows dec 1 st at each end of every row.
(39 (41:49:51) sts.)
Work 28 (28:32:34) rows dec 1 st at each end of next and
every foll alt row. (11 (13:17:17) sts.)
Leave rem 13 (11:17:17) sts on a holder.

NECKBAND & TIES

Sew in all ends.
Join raglan seams.
With RS facing, 3¼ mm (UK 10/US 3) needles and
Waterbaby, pick up and k 8 (10:10:14) sts evenly along neck
edge of Right Front, 11 (13:17:17) sts from holder at top of
Right Sleeve, 21 (25: 25: 27) sts from holder at Back Neck,
11 (13:17:17) sts from holder at top of Left Sleeve and
8 (10:10:14) sts evenly along neck edge of Left Front.
(59 (71: 79: 89) sts.)
Next row: Cast on and p 60 sts, p to end.
Next row: Cast on and k 60 sts, k to end.
(179 (191: 199: 209) sts.)
Beg with a p row, work 2 rows in st st.
Cast off p wise.

Allow the neckband and ties to curl back. Roll the edges of
the ties towards each other, so that the reverse side is
showing, and slip stitch together.

RIGHT FRONT TRIM

With RS facing, 3¼ mm (UK 10/US 3) needles and
Waterbaby, starting 4 rows up from the cast-on edge,
pick up and k 51 (57:71:75) sts evenly along front edge.
Beg with a p row, work 4 rows in st st. Cast off p wise.

LEFT FRONT TRIM

With RS facing, 3¼ mm (UK 10/US 3) needles and
Waterbaby, pick up and k 51 (57:71:75) sts evenly along
front edge, stopping 4 rows up from the cast-on edge.
Beg with a p row, work 4 rows in st st.
Cast off p wise.

Allow trims to roll towards right side of front. Sew top edge
of each trim to underside of each tie, and bottom edge to
rolled bottom edge of each front.

FLOWER (Make 2)

With 3¼ mm (UK 10/US 3) needles and Tulip cast on 35 sts.
Row 1: (RS) [K1, cast off 5 sts (2 sts left on RH needle)] to
end. (10 sts.)
Break yarn, thread through rem sts and draw up tightly.

Sew a French knot in Willow in the centre of each flower.

TO MAKE UP

Join side and underarm seams, reversing the seam for the
first 4 rows.
Sew flower to end of each tie.

Top tank tops

With pink hearts for the girls and blue stars for the boys, these tank tops will quickly become indispensable items in your child's wardrobe. Soft, fluffy, cute and very easy to wear.

FELTED KNITTING

SKILL LEVEL: **MODERATE**

MEASUREMENTS

Age	2–3	3–4	4–5	5–6	years
To fit chest	56	58	61	63	cm
	22	23	24	25	in
Actual width	60	64	66	70	cm
	23½	25	26½	27½	in
Actual length	36	38	40	42	cm
	14	15	15½	16½	in

In the instructions, figures are given for the smallest size first; larger sizes follow in brackets. Where only one set of figures is given this applies to all sizes.

MATERIALS
Girls/Hearts colour way

- 2 (2:3:3) x 25 g balls of Jamieson & Smith (Shetland Wool Brokers Ltd) 2 ply Jumper Weight in Dark Red/Claret 43 (A)
- 1 (2:2:3) x 25 g balls of Jamieson & Smith (Shetland Wool Brokers Ltd) 2 ply Jumper Weight in Pink Mixture FC22 (B)
- 2 (2:3:3) x 25 g balls of Jamieson & Smith (Shetland Wool Brokers Ltd) 2 ply Jumper Weight in Pink/Rose 101 (C)
- 2 x buttons

Boys/Stars colour way

- 2 (2:3:3) x 25 g balls of Jamieson & Smith (Shetland Wool Brokers Ltd) 2 ply Jumper Weight in Navy 21 (A)
- 1 (2:2:3) x 25 g balls of Jamieson & Smith (Shetland Wool Brokers Ltd) 2 ply Jumper Weight in Royal 18 (B)
- 2 (2:3:3) x 25 g balls of Jamieson & Smith (Shetland Wool Brokers Ltd) 2 ply Jumper Weight in Pale Blue 14 (C)
- 2 x buttons

For both colour ways

- Pair of 5 mm (UK 6/US 8) knitting needles

ABBREVIATIONS
See page 10

TENSION
Before machine felting:
19½ sts and 24 rows to 10 cm (4 in) measured over stocking stitch using 5 mm (UK 6/US 8) needles.
After machine felting (Method A):
20 sts and 36 rows to 10 cm (4 in) measured over stocking stitch.

front and back

TANK TOP

STRIPE SEQUENCE

Work 4 rows in C, 2 rows in A, 2 rows in B, 2 rows in A, 4 rows in C, 2 rows in B, 2 rows in A, 2 rows in B. These 20 rows form the stripe pattern.

BACK

(Boys and Girls versions both the same)

With 5 mm (UK6/US 8) needles and A cast on 60 (64:66:70) sts.

* Beg with a p row, work 4 rows in rev st st.

Change to B.

Next row: P0 (0:0:1), k0 (0:1:2), p0 (2:2:2), [k2, p2] to last 0 (2:3:5) sts, k0 (2:2:2), p0 (0:1:2), k0 (0:0:1).

Rep the last row 5 times more. *

Change to C and, beg with a k row, work 3 sets of the stripe sequence as set out above (60 rows).

Then work 4 (10:16:18) further rows of the stripe sequence.

SHAPE ARMHOLES

Keeping the stripe sequence as set cast off 2 sts at the beg of the next 4 rows. (52 (56:58:62) sts.)

Next row: Dec 1 st at each end of row. (50 (54:56:60) sts.) Beg with a p row, and keeping the stripe sequence as set, work 47 (47:49:55) rows straight.

SHAPE NECK AND SHOULDERS

Next row: K 14 (15:16:16), turn.

Work on these 14 (15:16:16) sts only as folls, keeping the stripe sequence as set.

Next row: Cast off 2 sts, p to end. (12 (13:14:14) sts.)

Next row: Cast off 6 (6:7:7) sts, k to last 2 sts, k2tog. (5 (6:6:6) sts.)

P 1 row.

Cast off the rem 5 (6:6:6) sts.

With RS facing rejoin yarn to rem sts and work as folls.

Cast off centre 22 (24:24:28) sts, k to end. (14 (15:16:16) sts.)

Work on these 14 (15:16:16) sts only as folls, keeping the stripe sequence as set.

P 1 row.

Next row: Cast off 2 sts, k to end. (12 (13:14:14) sts.)

Next row: Cast off 6 (6:7:7) sts, p to last 2 sts, p2tog. (5 (6:6:6) sts.)

Cast off the rem 5 (6:6:6) sts.

FRONT

With 5 mm (UK6/US 8) needles and A cast on 60 (64:66:70) sts.

Work as for Back from * to *

Change to C and, beg with a k row, work 4 rows in st st.

PLACE CHART

(For girls work from the Hearts Chart, for boys work from the Stars Chart)

Next row: K across the first row of the corresponding sized chart.

Beg with a p row, and using the intarsia method, work a further 59 (65:71:73) rows of the chart in st st.

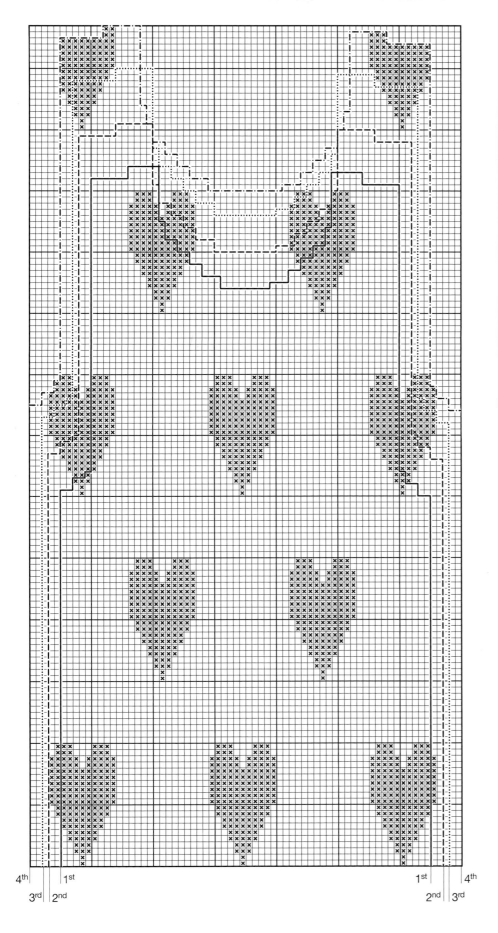

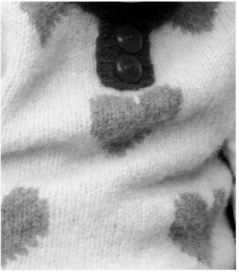

HEARTS CHART
KEY

☐   Rose

✕   Pink Mixture

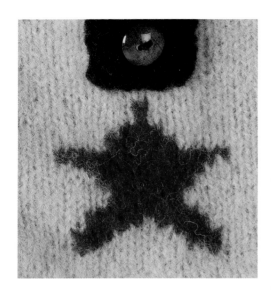

STARS CHART

KEY

☐ Pale Blue

- Royal

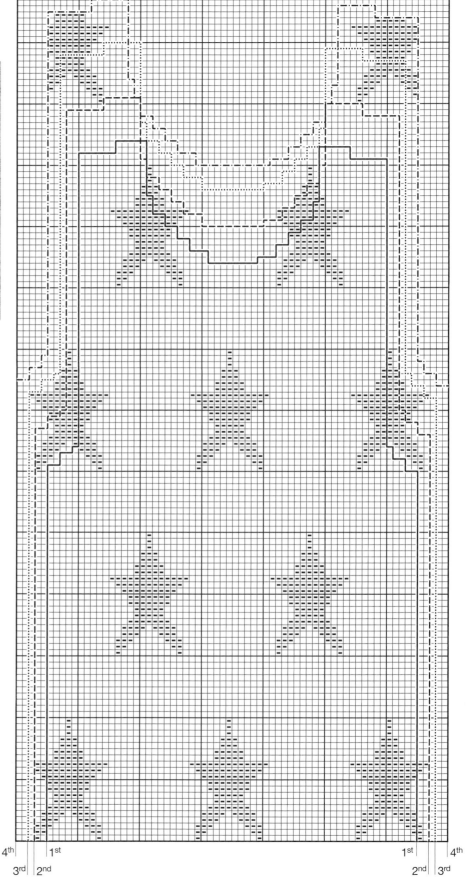

4th   1st   1st   4th

3rd 2nd   2nd 3rd

SHAPE ARMHOLES
Still working from the chart as set cast off 2 sts at the beg of the next 4 rows (52 (56:58:62) sts.)
Next row: Dec 1 st at each end of row. (50 (54:56:60) sts.)
Beg with a p row, and following the chart as set, work 29 (29:29:31) rows straight.

SHAPE NECK
Next row: K21 (22:23:24), turn.
Work on these 21 (22:23:24) sts only as folls, cont to follow the chart as set.
Next row: Cast off 3 sts, p to end. (18 (19:20:21) sts.)
K 1 row.

Cast off 2 sts at the beg of the next and foll 2 alt rows. (12 (13:14:15) sts.)
Work 2 rows in st st.
Next row: Dec 1 st at neck edge. (11 (12:13:14) sts.)
Work 2 rows in st st.
4th size only
Next row: Dec 1 st at neck edge. (13 sts.)
All sizes
Work 7 (7:9:12) rows in st st.

SHAPE SHOULDER
Next row: Cast off 6 (6:7:7) sts, k to end.
P 1 row.
Cast off the rem 5 (6:6:6) sts.
With RS facing rejoin yarn to rem sts and work as folls.
Cast off centre 8 (10:10:12) sts, k to end. (21 (22:23:24) sts.)
P 1 row.
Next row: Cast off 3 sts, k to end. (18 (19:20:21) sts.)
P 1 row.
Cast off 2 sts at the beg of the next and foll 2 alt rows. (12 (13:14:15) sts.)
Work 2 rows in st st.
Next row: Dec 1 st at neck edge. (11 (12:13:14) sts.)
Work 2 rows in st st.
4th size only
Next row: Dec 1 st at neck edge. (13 sts.)
All sizes
Work 7 (7:9:12) rows in st st.

SHAPE SHOULDER
Next row: Cast off 6 (6:7:7) sts, p to end.
K 1 row.
Cast off the rem 5 (6:6:6) sts.

PLACKET
With 5 mm (UK6/US 8) needles and A cast on 12 sts.
Next row: [K2, p2] to end.
Rep the last row 9 times more.
Cast off loosely.

NECK TRIM

With 5 mm (UK6/US 8) needles and A cast on
74 (76:82:88) sts.
Beg with a k row, work 8 rows in st st.
Cast off loosely.

ARMHOLE TRIM (Make 2)

With 5 mm (UK6/US 8) needles and A cast on
66 (66:72:76) sts.
Beg with a k row, work 8 rows in st st.
Cast off loosely.

FELTING INSTRUCTIONS

Work in all ends with a needle.
Following the instructions on page 14 for machine felting
Method A, wash all pieces together, placing the small items
in a mesh laundry bag, to felt.
Reshape whilst damp, dry thoroughly and repeat wash cycle
if necessary to achieve desired level of felting and correct
dimensions.

TO MAKE UP

With one short edge of placket level with neck edge, sew
placket to centre front.
Sew left shoulder seam. With the purl side of the neck trim
as the right side, sew one long edge of trim all around the
front and back neck, stretching to fit if necessary. Roll the
trim around the seam just made and sew the other edge of
trim to the other side of seam.
Sew the right shoulder seam and ends of neck trim ends.
Sew each armhole trim in the same way as the neck trim.
Sew side seams.
Sew buttons to placket.

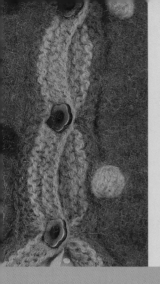

Sweetie

The felted bobbles on this cardigan remind me of sweets, hence the name.
An unashamedly girly cardigan bursting with texture; ideal for fun and frolics!

FELTED KNITTING

SKILL LEVEL: ADVANCED

MEASUREMENTS

Age	2–3	3–4	4–5	5–6	years
To fit chest	56	58	61	63	cm
	22	23	24	25	in
Actual width	61	66	72	76	cm
	24	26	28	30	in
Actual length	34	35	37	40	cm
	13½	14	14½	16½	in
Sleeve length	24	26	29	33	cm
	9½	10½	11½	13	in

In the instructions, figures are given for the smallest size first; larger sizes follow in brackets. Where only one set of figures is given this applies to all sizes.

MATERIALS

- 7 (7:8:9) x 25 g balls of Rowan Scottish Tweed 4 ply in Orange/Sunset 011
- 1 (1:1:2) x 25 g balls of Rowan Scottish Tweed 4 ply in Pink/Brilliant Pink 010
- 1 (1:1:2) x 25 g balls of Rowan Scottish Tweed 4 ply in Gold 028
- 1 x 25 g ball of Rowan Scottish Tweed 4 ply in Red/Lobster 017
- 1 x 25 g ball of Rowan Scottish Tweed 4 ply in Dark Red/Claret 013
- Pair of 5 mm (UK 6/US 8) knitting needles
- 3 x buttons

ABBREVIATIONS

MB = Make Bobble; see also page 10

TENSION

Before machine felting:
18½ sts and 24 rows to 10 cm (4 in) measured over stocking stitch using 5 mm (UK 6/US 8) needles.

After machine felting (Method A):
21 sts and 40 rows to 10 cm (4 in) measured over stocking stitch.

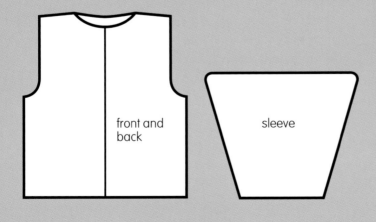

front and back

sleeve

CARDIGAN

MAKE BOBBLE (MB)

Join in col required.

Work into the front and back of the next st until there are 5 sts, turn.

Beg with a p row, work 4 rows in st st on these 5 sts only.

Next row: P2tog, p1, p2tog.

Next row: With Orange, k3tog, cont along row as instructions state.

BACK

With 5 mm (UK 6/US 8) needles and Pink cast on 63 (69:75:79) sts.

* Working in gst (k every row), k 2 rows Pink, 2 rows Gold and 2 rows Orange.

Beg with a k row, work 10 rows in st st. *

BOBBLE PATTERN

Next row: K3 (6:9:11), MB Pink, k13, MB Red, k13, MB Gold, k13, MB Claret, k13, MB Pink, k3 (6:9:11).

Beg with a p row, work 17 rows in st st.

Next row: 4th size only: K4, MB Gold.

All sizes

K10 (13:16:13), MB Claret, k13, MB Pink, k13, MB Red, k13, MB Gold, k10 (13:16:13).

4th size only

MB Claret, k4.

Beg with a p row, work 17 rows in st st.

These 36 rows form the bobble pattern.

Keeping the bobbles placed on the same sts throughout, cont as follows.

Work 14 (16:22:26) more rows of bobble pattern.

SHAPE ARMHOLES

Cast off 2 sts at beg of next 2 rows.

Next row: Dec 1 st at each end of row. (57 (63:69:73) sts.)

Beg with a p row, and keeping bobble pattern as set, work 68 (67:73:81) rows straight.

SHAPE SHOULDERS AND NECK

Next row: K15 (17:19:20), turn.

Cast off 3 sts at beg of next 2 rows. (9 (11:13:14) sts.)

Next row: Dec 1 st at beg of row, p to end.

Cast off rem 8 (10:12:13) sts.

With RS facing, rejoin yarn to rem sts and cont as follows.

Next row: Cast off 27 (29:31:33) sts, k to end.

Cast off 3 sts at beg of next 2 rows. (9 (11:13:14) sts.)

Next row: Dec 1 st at end of row.

Cast off rem 8 (10:12:13) sts.

LEFT FRONT

With 5 mm (UK 6/US 8) needles and Pink cast on 33 (36:38:40) sts.

Work as for back from * to *.

BOBBLE PATTERN

Next row: K2 (5:7:9), MB Pink, k13, MB Red, k13, MB Gold, k2.

Beg with a p row, work 17 rows in st st.

Next row: 4th size only: K2, MB Gold.

All sizes

K9 (12:14:13), MB Claret, k13, MB Pink, k9.

Beg with a p row, work 17 rows in st st.

These 36 rows form the bobble pattern.

Keeping the bobbles placed on the same sts throughout, cont as follows.

Work 14 (16:22:26) more rows of bobble pattern.

SHAPE ARMHOLE

Next row: Cast off 2 sts, k to end.

P 1 row.

Next row: Dec 1 st at armhole edge. (30 (33:35:37) sts.)

Beg with a p row, and keeping bobble pattern as set, work 56 (58:60:62) rows straight.

SHAPE NECK

Next row: Cast off 6 sts, p to end. (24 (27:29:31) sts.)
K 1 row.
Cast off 2 sts at beg of next and foll 5 (5:5:6) alt rows.
(12 (15:17:17) sts.)
Beg with a k row work 0 (0:2:6) rows in st st.

SHAPE SHOULDER

** **Next row:** Cast off 3 sts at beg of row.
Next row: Dec 1 st at neck edge.
Cast off rem 8 (11:13:13) sts. **

RIGHT FRONT

With 5 mm (UK 6/US 8) needles and Pink cast on
33 (36:38:40) sts.
Work as for back from * to *.

BOBBLE PATTERN

Next row: K2, MB Claret, k13, MB Pink, k13, MB Red, k2
(5:7:9).
Beg with a p row, work 17 rows in st st.
Next row: K9, MB Red, k13, MB Gold, k9 (12:14:13),
4th size only MB Claret, k2.
All sizes
Beg with a p row, work 17 rows in st st.
These 36 rows form the bobble pattern.
Keeping the bobbles placed on the same sts throughout,
cont as follows.
Work 15 (17:23:27) more rows of bobble pattern.

SHAPE ARMHOLE

Next row: Cast off 2 sts, p to end.
Next row: Dec 1 st at armhole edge. (30 (33:35:37) sts.)
Beg with a p row, and keeping bobble pattern as set, work
57 (59:61:63) rows straight.

SHAPE NECK

Next row: Cast off 6 sts, k to end. (24 (27:29:31) sts.)
P 1 row.

Cast off 2 sts at beg of next and foll 5 (5:5:6) alt rows.
(12 (15:17:17) sts.)
Beg with a p row work 1 (1:3:7) rows in st st.

SHAPE SHOULDER

Work as for Left Front from ** to **.

SLEEVE (Make 2)

With 5 mm (UK 6/US 8) needles and Pink cast on
33 (35:37:39) sts.
Working in gst (k every row), k 2 rows Pink, 2 rows Gold and
2 rows Orange.
Beg with a k row, work 10 rows in st st, inc 1 st at each end
of 6th row. (35 (37:39:41) sts.)

BOBBLE PATTERN

Next row: K10 (11:12:13), MB Gold, k13, MB Claret, k10 (11:12:13).

Beg with a p row, work 17 rows in st st, inc 1 st at each end of 1st, 7th and 13th of these rows. (41 (43:45:47) sts.)

Next row: K6 (7:8:9), MB Pink, k13, MB Red, k13, MB Gold, k6 (7:8:9).

Beg with a p row, work 17 rows in st st, inc 1 st at each end of 1st, 7th and 13th of these rows. (47 (49:51:53) sts.)
These 36 rows form the bobble pattern.
Keeping the bobbles placed on the same sts throughout, and incorporating new bobbles into sleeve as sts inc, cont inc at each end of 2nd every foll 6th row to 63 (67:71:75) sts.
Cont bobble pattern without shaping for a further 2 (6:12:22) rows.

SHAPE TOP

Cast off 2 sts at beg of next 2 rows.

Next row: Dec 1 st at each end of row. (57 (61:65:69) sts.)
P 1 row.
Cast off.

POCKET (Make 2)

With 5 mm (UK 6/US 8) needles and Orange cast on 19 sts.
Beg with a k row, work 36 rows in st st.

BOBBLE EDGING

Next row: Cast off 3 sts, MB Pink, cast off 4 sts, MB Red, cast off 4 sts, MB Gold, cast off 4 sts, MB Claret, cast off 4 sts.

NECK TRIM

With 5 mm (UK 6/US 8) needles and Orange cast on 79 (80:84:84) sts.
K 6 rows.

BOBBLE EDGING

Next row: Cast off 3 (4:6:6) sts, [MB Pink, cast off 4 sts, MB Red, cast off 4 sts, MB Gold, cast off 4 sts, MB Claret, cast off 4 sts] 4 times, MB Pink, cast off 4 sts, MB Red, cast off 4 sts, MB Gold, cast off 4 (4:6:6) sts.

BUTTON BAND

With 5 mm (UK 6/US 8) needles and Pink cast on 64 (67:70:75) sts.
Working in gst (k every row), k 2 rows Pink, 2 rows Gold and 2 rows Orange.
Cast off.

BUTTONHOLE BAND

With 5 mm (UK 6/US 8) needles and Pink cast on 64 (67:70:75) sts.
Working in gst (k every row), k 2 rows Pink.
Change to Gold.

Next row: K4, [yfwd, k2tog, k8 (10:12:14)] twice, yfwd, k2tog, k to end.
K 1 row Gold, 2 rows Orange.
Cast off.

FELTING INSTRUCTIONS

Work in all ends with a needle.
Following the instructions on page 14 for machine felting Method A, wash all pieces together, placing the small items in a mesh laundry bag, to felt.
Reshape whilst damp, dry thoroughly and repeat wash cycle if necessary to achieve desired level of felting and correct dimensions.

TO MAKE UP

Join shoulder seams.
Sew sleeve head to armholes. Sew underarm and side seams of back and fronts.
Sew button band and buttonhole band to fronts.
Sew neck trim to neck edge.
Sew a pocket to each front.
Sew on buttons to correspond with buttonholes.

Perfect pea coat

The yarn used for this coat felts beautifully to produce a wonderfully soft and very resilient garment. The addition of brightly coloured stitching and contrast buttons set it apart from the rest. A practical pea coat; perfect in every way!

FELTED KNITTING

SKILL LEVEL: MODERATE ★ ★ ☆

MEASUREMENTS

Age	2–3	3–4	4–5	5–6	years
To fit chest	56	58	61	63	cm
	22	23	24	25	in
Actual width	68	72	74	76	cm
	26½	28½	29	30	in
Actual length	39	40	43	45	cm
	15½	16	17	18	in
Sleeve length	33	36	37	38	cm
	13	14	14½	15	in

In the instructions, figures are given for the smallest size first; larger sizes follow in brackets. Where only one set of figures is given this applies to all sizes.

MATERIALS

- 11 (12:13:13) x 25 g balls of Rowan Scottish Tweed 4ply in Navy/Winter Navy 021
- Pair of 5 mm (UK 6/US 8) knitting needles
- 10 x buttons
- 1 x skein of DMC stranded cotton embroidery thread in Green 702

ABBREVIATIONS

See page 10

TENSION

Before machine felting:

18 sts and 24 rows to 10 cm (4 in) measured over stocking stitch using 5 mm (UK 6/US 8) needles.

After machine felting (Method A):

25 sts and 40 rows to 10 cm (4 in) measured over stocking stitch.

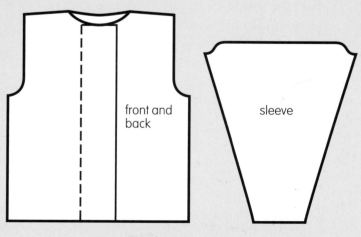

front and back

sleeve

COAT

BACK

With 5 mm (UK 6/US 8) needles and Navy cast on
85 (90:92:95) sts.
Beg with a k row, work in st st until back meas
40 (41.5:45:47.5) cm (15½ (16:17½:18½) in) ending with a
WS row.

SHAPE ARMHOLES

Cast off 2 sts at beg of next 2 rows. (81 (86:88:91) sts.)
Dec 1 st at each end of next 2 rows. (77 (82:84:87) sts.)
Beg with a k row, work in st st without shaping until armhole
meas 24 (25.5:26.5:28) cm (9½ (10:10½:11) in) ending with a
WS row.

SHAPE SHOULDERS AND NECK

Next row: Cast off 5, k12 (14:15:15), k2tog, turn.
Work on these 14 (16:17:17) sts only as follows.
Next row: Cast off 2 sts, p to end. (12 (14:15:15) sts.)
Next row: Cast off 6 (6:7:7), k3 (5:5:5), k2tog. (5 (7:7:7) sts.)
Next row: P2tog, p to end.
Cast off rem 4 (6:6:6) sts.
With RS facing rejoin yarn to rem sts and cont as follows.
Cast off centre 37 (38:38:41) sts, k to end.
Work on these 20 (22:23:23) sts only as follows.
Next row: Cast off 5, p12 (14:15:15), p2tog.
(14 (16:17:17) sts.)
Next row: Cast off 2 sts, k to end. (12 (14:15:15) sts.)
Next row: Cast off 6 (6:7:7), p3 (5:5:5), p2tog.
(5 (7:7:7) sts.)
Next row: K2tog, k to end.
Cast off rem 4 (6:6:6) sts.

LEFT FRONT

With 5 mm (UK 6/US 8) needles and Navy cast on
52 (55:56:57) sts.
Beg with a k row, work in st st until front meas
40 (41.5:45:47.5) cm (15½ (16:17½:18½) in) ending with a
WS row.

SHAPE ARMHOLE

Next row: Cast off 2 sts, k to end. (50 (53:54:55) sts.)
Next row: P to last 2 sts, p2tog.
Next row: K2tog, k to end. (48 (51:52:53) sts.)
Beg with a p row, work in st st without shaping until armhole
meas 15 (16.5:17.5:19) cm (6 (6½:7:7½) in) ending with a
RS row.

SHAPE NECK

Next row: Cast off 18 (19:20:20) sts, p to end.
(30 (32:32:33) sts.)
Dec 1 st at neck edge on next and foll 9 alt rows.
(20 (22:22:23) sts.)
P 1 row.

SHAPE SHOULDER

Next row: Cast off 5, k12 (14:14:15), k2tog. (14 (16:16:17)
sts.)
Next row: Cast off 2 sts, p to end. (12 (14:14:15) sts.)
Next row: Cast off 6 (6:6:7), k3 (5:5:5), k2tog. (5 (7:7:7) sts.)
Next row: P2tog, p to end.
Cast off rem 4 (6:6:6) sts.

RIGHT FRONT

With 5 mm (UK 6/US 8) needles and Navy cast on
52 (55:56 :57) sts.
Beg with a k row, work in st st until front meas
9 (11.5:14:17.5) cm (3½ (4½:5½:7) in) ending with a WS row.
Buttonhole row 1: K4, cast off 2 sts, k9, cast off 2 sts, k to
end.
Buttonhole row 2: P34 (37:38:39), cast on 2 sts, p10, cast
on 2 sts, p to end.
These 2 rows form buttonhole pair. Work 3 further pairs of
buttonholes in the same way every 15 cm (6 in) **at the same
time** work in st st until front meas 40 (41.5:45:47.5) cm
(15½ (16:17½:18½) in) ending with a RS row.

SHAPE ARMHOLE

Next row: Cast off 2 sts, p to end. (50 (53:54:55) sts.)
Next row: K to last 2 sts, k2tog.
Next row: P2tog, p to end. (48 (51:52:53) sts.)

Beg with a k row, work in st st, cont to place buttonholes in same positions as required, until armhole meas 15 (16.5:16.5:19) cm (6 (6½:7:7½) in) ending with a WS row.

SHAPE NECK
Next row: Cast off 18 (19:20:20) sts, k to end.
(30 (32:32:33) sts.)
Dec 1 st at neck edge on next and foll 9 alt rows.
(20 (22:22:23) sts.)
K 1 row.

SHAPE SHOULDER
Next row: Cast off 5, p12 (14:14:15), p2tog.
(14 (16:16:17) sts.)
Next row: Cast off 2 sts, k to end. (12 (14:14:15) sts.)
Next row: Cast off 6 (6:6:7), p3 (5:5:5), p2tog. (5 (7:7:7) sts.)
Next row: K2tog, k to end.
Cast off rem 4 (6:6:6) sts.

SLEEVE (Make 2)
With 5 mm (UK 6/US 8) needles and Navy cast on
47 (50:52:55) sts.
Beg with a k row, work in st st inc 1 st at each end of every
9th (9th:10th:10th) row to 75 (78:80:83) sts.
Beg with a k row, work 0 (12:2:6) rows in st st without shaping.

SHAPE TOP
Cast off 2 sts at beg of next 2 rows. (71 (74:76:79) sts.)
Dec 1 st at each end of next 4 rows.
Cast off rem 63 (66:68:71) sts.

COLLAR
With 5 mm (UK 6/US 8) needles and Navy cast on
100 (103:106:109) sts.
Beg with a k row, work 8 (10:12:12) rows in st st.
Next row: K2, m1, k to last 2 sts, m1, k2.
P 1 row.
Rep the last 2 rows 3 (4:5:5) times more.
(108 (113:118:121) sts.)
Cast off 2 sts at beg of next 4 rows. (100 (105:110:113) sts.)

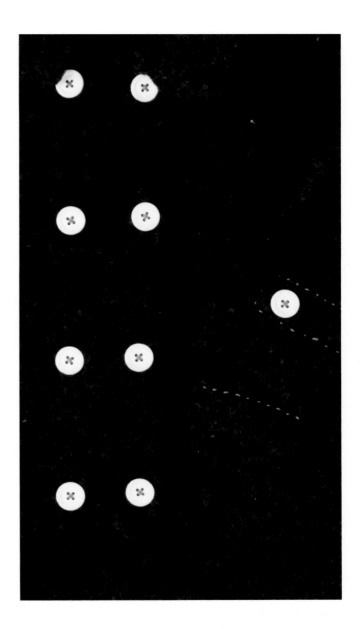

Dec 1 st at each end of next and foll alt row.
(96 (101:106:109) sts.)
P 1 row.
Cast off.

POCKET TRIM (Make 2)
With 5 mm (UK 6/US 8) needles and Navy cast on
20 (20:23:23) sts.
Beg with a k row, work 12 rows in st st.
Cast off.

SLEEVE TRIMS (Make 2)

With 5 mm (UK 6/US 8) needles and Navy cast on
32 (35:37:40) sts.
Beg with a k row, work 12 rows in st st.
Cast off.

FELTING INSTRUCTIONS

Work in all ends with a needle.
Following the instructions on page 14 for machine felting
Method A, wash all pieces together, placing the small items
in a mesh laundry bag, to felt.
Reshape whilst damp, dry thoroughly and repeat wash cycle
if necessary to achieve desired level of felting and correct
dimensions.

TO MAKE UP

Join shoulder seams.
Sew sleeve head to armholes. Sew underarm and side
seams of back and fronts.
Fold collar in half and place the centre point at the centre of
back neck and each end approximately 6 cm (2½ in) from
each front edge. Sew lower edge of collar to neck edge of
coat.
Sew on buttons with green embroidery thread to correspond
with buttonholes in right front.
Sew running stitch in green thread along the top edge of
each pocket flap. Sew pocket flaps to fronts at a slight angle.
Sew running stitch in green thread along the top, bottom
and side edges of each sleeve trim. Sew sleeve trim to top of
sleeve approximately 4 cm (1½ in) from lower edge. Sew a
button to one end of sleeve trim.

Jurassic jacket

Just the thing for any budding palaeontologists! The random colour effect of this yarn perfectly evokes nature and the spike trim running down the hood and back is just too cute...

FELTED KNITTING

SKILL LEVEL: **MODERATE**

MEASUREMENTS

Age	2–3	3–4	4–5	5–6	years
To fit chest	56	58	61	63	cm
	22	23	24	25	in
Actual width	61	66	71	76	cm
	24	26	28	30	in
Actual length	38.5	40	42	46	cm
	15	16	16½	18	in
Sleeve length	24	26.5	29.5	33	cm
	9½	10½	11½	13	in

In the instructions, figures are given for the smallest size first; larger sizes follow in brackets. Where only one set of figures is given this applies to all sizes.

MATERIALS

- 5 (6:6:7) x 50 g balls of Twilleys of Stamford Freedom Spirit in Green Mix/Nature 514
- 1 (1:1:2) x 50 g balls of Twilleys of Stamford Freedom Spirit in Brown Mix/Earth 505
- Pair of 5 mm (UK 6/US 8) knitting needles
- 30 cm (12 in) (34 cm (13 in): 36 cm (14 in): 40 cm (16 in) long open ended zip or length appropriate for finished garment

ABBREVIATIONS

See page 10

TENSION

Before machine felting:

18½ sts and 28 rows to 10 cm (4 in) measured over stocking stitch using 5 mm (UK 6/US 8) needles.
18 sts and 28 rows to 10 cm (4 in) measured over moss stitch using 5 mm (UK 6/US 8) needles.

After machine felting (Method B):

20 sts and 32 rows to 10 cm (4 in) measured over stocking stitch.

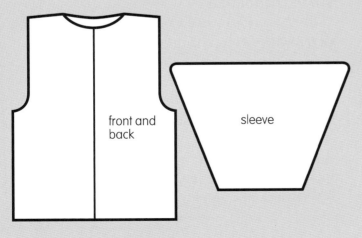

front and back

sleeve

JACKET

BACK
With 5 mm (UK 6/US 8) needles and Brown Mix cast on 61 (66:71:76) sts.
K 4 rows.
Change to Green Mix and, beg with a k row, work 62 (64:68:72) rows in st st.

SHAPE ARMHOLES
Cast off 2 sts at beg of next 2 rows.
Next row: Dec 1 st at each end of row. (55 (60:65:70) sts.)
Beg with a p row, work 51 (55:57:65) rows in st st.

SHAPE SHOULDERS AND NECK
Next row: K14 (16:18:20), turn.
Work on these 14 (16:18:20) sts only as follows.
Cast off 3 sts at beg of next 2 rows.
Next row: Dec 1 st at beg of row.
Cast off rem 7 (9:11:13) sts.
With RS facing rejoin yarn to rem sts and cont as follows.
Cast off 27 (28:29:30) sts, k to end.
Cast off 3 sts at beg of next 2 rows.

Next row: Dec 1 st at end of row.
Cast off rem 7 (9:11:13) sts.

LEFT FRONT
With 5 mm (UK 6/US 8) needles and Brown Mix cast on 30 (32:35:37) sts.
* K 4 rows.
Change to Green Mix.
K 1 row. *
Next row: K2, p to end.
Rep the last 2 rows, keeping the 2 sts at left edge k every row, until 62 (64:68:72) rows have been worked.

SHAPE ARMHOLE
Next row: Cast off 2 sts, k to end.
Next row: K2, p to end.
Next row: Dec 1 st at beg of row. (27 (29:32:34) sts.)
Beg with a p row, work 42 (44:44:52) rows straight.

SHAPE NECK
Next row: Cast off 3 sts, p to end. (24 (26:29:31) sts.)
Dec 1 st at neck edge on next 7 (7:8:8) rows.
(17 (19:21:23) sts.)
3rd & 4th sizes only
K 1 row.
All sizes
Next row: Cast off 3 sts, p to end. (14 (16:18:20) sts.)
Beg with a k row work 0 (2:2:2) rows in st st.

SHAPE SHOULDER
Cast off 3 sts at beg of next 2 rows.
Next row: Dec 1 st at neck edge.
P 1 row. Cast off rem 7 (9:11:13) sts.

RIGHT FRONT
With 5 mm (UK 6/US 8) needles and Brown Mix cast on 30 (32:35:37) sts.
Work as for left front from * to *.
Next row: P to last 2 sts, k2.
Rep the last 2 rows, keeping the 2 sts at right edge k every row, until 63 (65:69:73) rows have been worked.

SHAPE ARMHOLE

Next row: Cast off 2 sts, p to last 2 sts, k2.

K 1 row.

Next row: Dec 1 st at beg of row. (27 (29:32:34) sts.)

Beg with a k row, work 42 (44:44:52) rows straight.

SHAPE NECK

Next row: Cast off 3 sts, k to end. (24 (26:29:31) sts.)

Dec 1 st at neck edge on next 7 (7:8:8) rows.

(17 (19:21:23) sts.)

3rd & 4th sizes only

P 1 row.

All sizes

Next row: Cast off 3 sts, k to end. (14 (16:18:20) sts.)

Beg with a p row work 0 (2:2:2) rows in st st.

SHAPE SHOULDER

Cast off 3 sts at beg of next 2 rows.

Dec 1 st at neck edge.

Cast off rem 7 (9:11:13) sts.

SLEEVE (Make 2)

With 5 mm (UK 6/US 8) needles and Brown Mix cast on 32 (34:36:38) sts.

K 4 rows.

Change to Green Mix and, beg with a k row, work in st st inc 1 st at each end of every 4th row to 68 (72:76:86) sts.

Beg with a k row, work 0 (4:10:4) rows in st st without shaping.

SHAPE TOP

Cast off 3 sts at beg of next 2 rows.

Next row: Dec 1 st at each end of row. (60 (64:68:78) sts.)

P 1 row.

Cast off.

LEFT HOOD

With 5 mm (UK 6/US 8) needles and Green Mix cast on 3 sts.

Row 1: K

Row 2: K2, p to last st, inc 1.

Row 3: Inc 1, k to end.

Rep rows 2 and 3, 3 times more, then the 2nd row once more. (12 sts)

Next row: Cast on 3 sts, k to end. (15 sts)

Next row: K2, p to end.

Next row: Cast on 21 (23:25:27) sts, k to end.

(36 (38:40:42) sts.)

Beg with a p row, work 25 rows in st st, keeping the 2 sts at the left front opening edge k every row and inc 1 st at right back edge on every 6th row. (40 (42:44:46) sts.)

Beg with a k row, work 22 (28:32:36) rows straight without shaping.

Next row: Skpo, k to end.

Next row: K2, p to end.

Rep the last 2 rows, 5 times more. (34 (36:38:40) sts.)

Next row: Cast off 2 sts, k to end.

Next row: K2, p to end.

Rep the last 2 rows, 3 times more. (26 28:30:32) sts)

Next row: Cast off 3 sts, k to end.

Next row: K2, p to end.

Rep the last 2 rows, once more. (20 (22:24:26) sts)

Next row: Cast off 4 sts, k to end.

Next row: K2, p to end.

Next row: Cast off rem 16 (18:20:22) sts.

RIGHT HOOD

With 5 mm (UK 6/US 8) needles and Green Mix cast on 3 sts.

Row 1: K

Row 2: Inc 1, p to last 2 sts, k2.

Row 3: K to last st, inc 1.

Rep rows 2 and 3, 3 times more, then the 2nd row once more. (12 sts)

K 1 row.

Next row: Cast on 3 sts, p to last 2 sts, k2. (15 sts)

Next row: K 1 row.

Next row: Cast on 21 (23:25:27) sts, p to last 2 sts, k2. (36 (38:40:42) sts.)

Beg with a k row, work 24 rows in st st, keeping the 2 sts at the right front opening edge k every row and inc 1 st at left back edge on every 6th row. (40 (42:44:46) sts.)

Beg with a k row, work 23 (29:33:37) rows straight without shaping.

Next row: P2tog, p to last 2 sts, k2.

Next row: K.

Rep the last 2 rows, 5 times more. (34 (36:38:40) sts.)

Next row: Cast off 2 sts, p to last 2 sts, k2.

Next row: K.

Rep the last 2 rows, 3 times more. (26 28:30:32) sts.)

Next row: Cast off 3 sts, p to last 2 sts, k2.

Next row: K.

Rep the last 2 rows, once more. (20 (22:24:26) sts.)

Next row: Cast off 4 sts, p to last 2 sts, k2.

Next row: K.

Next row: Cast off rem 16 (18:20:22) sts.

SPIKE TRIM

With 5 mm (UK 6/US 8) needles and Brown Mix cast on 140 (150:160:170) sts.

Next row (RS): [K1, p1] to end.

Next row: [P1, k1] to end.

These 2 rows form moss st. Cont in moss st throughout.

Row 3: ** Work 10, turn.

Work on these 10 sts as follows:

Work 3 rows in moss st.

Row 7: P2tog, work 6, k2tog.

Next and every foll alt row: Work 1 row.

Row 9: K2tog, work 4, p2tog.

Row 11: P2tog, work 2, k2tog.

Row 13: K2tog, p2tog.

Row 14: K2tog, break yarn and thread through rem st. **

With RS facing, rejoin yarn to rem sts and rep from ** to ** 13 (14:15:16) times more.

FELTING INSTRUCTIONS

Work in all ends with a needle.

Following the instructions on page 15 for machine felting Method B, wash all pieces together, placing the spike trim in a mesh laundry bag, to felt.

Reshape whilst damp and dry thoroughly.

TO MAKE UP

Sew fronts to back at shoulder seams. Sew sleeve heads into armholes. Sew side and underarm seams.

Place right sides of hood together and, trapping spike trim between the two layers, sew through all layers.

Sew bottom edge of hood to neck edge matching shaping.

Sew remainder of spike trim down centre of back.

Sew zip between fronts.

Princess cape

Knitted from luxurious alpaca yarn, this little felted cape would look lovely
worn over a party dress or bridesmaid's dress. The satin bias binding,
organza ribbon and metallic thread embroidery give it a vintage charm.

FELTED KNITTING   **SKILL LEVEL: MODERATE**

MEASUREMENTS

Age	2–4	4–6	years
To fit chest	56–58	61–63	cm
	22–23	24–25	in
Actual width	40	45	cm
(bottom edge)	15½	17½	in
Actual length	25	29	cm
	10	11½	in

In the instructions, figures are given for the smaller size first;
larger size follows in brackets. Where only one set of figures
is given this applies to both sizes.

MATERIALS

- 4 x 50 g balls of UK Alpaca Super Fine Natural Double
  Knit in Cream/Parchment
- Pair of 4½ mm (UK 7/US 7) knitting needles
- 80 cm (32 in) Satin edged Organza Ribbon 22 mm
  (⅞ in) wide
- 60 cm (24 in) satin bias binding
- 1 x skein of DMC Light Effects embroidery thread in
  Gold E3821

ABBREVIATIONS

See page 10

TENSION

Before machine felting:
20 sts and 25 rows to 10 cm (4 in) measured over stocking
stitch using 4½ mm (UK 7/US 7) needles.
After machine felting (Method C):
27 sts and 34 rows to 10 cm (4 in) measured over stocking
stitch.

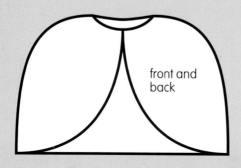
front and
back

CAPE

BACK

With 4½ mm (UK 7/US 7) needles and Cream cast on
108 (122) sts.
Beg with a k row, work 30 (32) rows in st st.
Dec 1 st at each end of next and every foll 4th row until
80 (88) sts rem.
P 1 row.

SHAPE SHOULDERS AND NECK

Next row: Cast off 7 (8) sts, k14 (15), turn.
Work on these 15 (16) sts only as follows.
Next row: P2tog, p to end. (14 (15) sts.)
Next row: Cast off 7 (8) sts, k to end. (7 sts.)
Next row: P2tog, p to end. (6 sts.)
Cast off rem 6 (6) sts.
With RS facing, rejoin yarn to rem sts and work as follows.
Next row: Cast off 36 (40) sts, k to end. (22 (24) sts.)
Next row: Cast off 7 (8) sts, p to end. (15 (16) sts.)
Next row: Skpo, k to end. (14 (15) sts.)
Next row: Cast off 7 (8) sts, p to end. (7 sts.)
Next row: Skpo, k to end. (6 sts.)
Cast off rem 6 (6) sts.

RIGHT FRONT

With 4½ mm (UK 7/US 7) needles and Cream cast on
20 (28) sts.
Beg with a k row, work 2 rows in st st.
Next row: Cast on 2 sts, k to end. (22 (30) sts.)
P 1 row.
Rep the last 2 rows to 36 (44) sts, ending with a p row.
Next row: Inc in 1st st, k to end. (37 (45) sts.)
P 1 row.
Rep the last 2 rows to 42 (51) sts.
Next row: Inc in 1st st, k to last 2 sts, k2tog. (42 (51) sts.)
P 1 row.
Next row: Inc in 1st st, k to end. (43 (52) sts.)
P 1 row.
Rep last 4 rows 4 (5) times. (47 (57) sts.)

Next row: Inc in 1st st, k to last 2 sts, k2tog. (43 (52) sts.)
Then cont to dec 1 st at left edge on every 4th row as set
until 43 (51) sts rem.
Beg with a p row, work 3 rows in st st.

SHAPE NECK

Next row: Cast off 6 (9) sts, k to last 2 sts, k2tog.
(36 (41) sts.)
P 1 row.
Next row: Cast off 3 (4) sts, k to end. (33 (37) sts.)
P 1 row.
Next row: Cast off 3 (4) sts, k to last 2 sts, k2tog.
(29 (32) sts.)
P 1 row.
Next row: Cast off 2 (3) sts, k to end. (27 (29) sts.)
P 1 row.
Next row: Skpo, k to last 2 sts, k2tog. (25 (27) sts.)
P 1 row.
Next row: Skpo, k to end. (24 (26) sts.)
P 1 row.
Next row: Skpo, k to last 2 sts, k2tog. (22 (24) sts.)

SHAPE SHOULDER

Next row: Cast off 7 (8) sts, p to end. (15 (16) sts.)
Next row: Skpo, k to end. (14 (15) sts.)
Next row: Cast off 7 (8) sts, p to end. (7 sts.)
Next row: Skpo, k to end. (6 sts.)
Cast off rem 6 (6) sts.

LEFT FRONT

With 4½ mm (UK 7/US 7) needles and Cream cast on
20 (28) sts.
K 1 row.
Next row: Cast on 2 sts, p to end. (22 (30) sts.)
K 1 row.
Rep the last 2 rows to 36 (44) sts.
P 1 row.
Next row: K to last 2 sts, inc1, k1. (37 (45) sts.)
P 1 row.
Rep the last 2 rows to 42 (51) sts, ending with a p row.
Next row: Skpo, k to last 2 sts, inc1, k1. (42 (51) sts.)

Next row: Cast off 3 (4) sts, p to end. (33 (37) sts.)
K 1 row.
Next row: Cast off 3 (4) sts, p to end. (30 (33) sts.)
Next row: Skpo, k to end. (29 (32) sts.)
Next row: Cast off 2 (3) sts, p to end. (27 (29) sts.) K 1 row.
Next row: P2tog, p to end. (26 (28) sts.) K 1 row.
Next row: K2tog, k to end. (25 (27) sts.)
Next row: P2tog, p to end. (24 (26) sts.) K1 row.
Next row: P2tog, p to end. (23 (25) sts.)
Next row: K2tog, k to end. (22 (24) sts.)
Next row: P2tog, p to end. (21 (23) sts.)

SHAPE SHOULDER
Next row: Cast off 7 (8) sts, k to end. (14 (15) sts.)
Next row: P2tog, p to end. (13 (14) sts.)
Next row: Cast off 7 (8) sts, k to end. (7 (7) sts.)
Cast off rem 6 sts.

FELTING INSTRUCTIONS
Work in all ends with a needle.
Following the instructions on page 15 for machine felting
Method C, wash all pieces together to felt.
Reshape whilst damp and dry thoroughly.

TO MAKE UP
Sew each front section to back at sides and shoulder,
curving seam.
Sew satin bias binding around neck edge.
Cut ribbon in half and sew one end of each half behind the
edge of each front just below bias binding.
Using 2 strands of Light Effects gold embroidery thread sew
lazy daisy stitches (see page 17) close to edges of front and
along lower edge of back about 3 cm (1¼ in) apart.

P 1 row.
Next row: K to last 2 sts, inc1 , k1. (43 (52) sts.)
P 1 row.
Next row: Skpo, k to last 2 sts, inc1, k1. (47 (57) sts.)
Rep last 4 rows 4 (5) times. (47(57)sts.)
Then cont to dec 1 st at right edge on every 4th row as set
until 43 (51) sts rem.
Beg with a p row, work 2 rows in st st.

SHAPE NECK
Next row: Cast off 6 (9) sts, p to end. (37 (42) sts.)
Next row: Skpo, k to end. (36 (41) sts.)

Useful addresses

YARN SUPPLIERS

As hand knitting yarns are largely fashion led, yarns and colours which are in a shade card one year may not be in there the following year. Therefore, please check yarn availability and stockists with the following suppliers.

Jamieson & Smith (Shetland Wool Brokers Ltd)

90 North Road
Lerwick
Shetland Isles
ZE1 0PQ
Tel: +44 (0) 1595 693579
Fax: +44 (0) 1595 695009
www.shetland-wool-brokers.zetnet.co.uk
E-mail:
sales@shetlandwoolbrokers.co.uk
Worldwide mail order available direct

Rowan & RYC

Green Lane Mill
Holmfirth
West Yorkshire
England
HD9 2DX
Tel: +44 (0) 1484 681881
Fax: +44 (0) 1484 687920
www.knitrowan.com
www.ryclassic.com
E-mail: mail@knitrowan.com
E-mail: info@ryclassic.com
Contact for stockists or order online

Sirdar

Sirdar Spining Ltd
Flanshaw Lane,
Alverthorpe
Wakefield
West Yorkshire
WF2 9ND
Tel: +44 (0) 1924 371501
Fax: +44 (0) 1924 290506
www.sirdar.co.uk
E-mail: consumer@sirdar.co.uk

Twilleys of Stamford

Roman Mill
Little Casterton Road
Stamford
Lincs
PE9 1BG
Tel: +44 (0) 1780 752661
Fax: +44 (0) 1780 765215
www.tbramsden.co.uk
E-mail: twilleys@tbramsden.co.uk

UK Alpaca Ltd

Vulscombe Farm
Pennymoor
Tiverton
Devon
EX16 8NB
Tel: +44 (0) 1598 753644
or: +44 (0) 1884 243579
www.ukalpaca.com
E-mail: info@ukalpaca.com
Worldwide mail order available direct

OTHER MATERIALS

DMC Creative World Ltd

1st Floor Compass Building
Feldspar Close
Warren Park
Enderby
Leicester
LE19 4SD
Telephone: +44 (0) 116 275 4000
Fax: +44 (0) 116 275 4020
www.dmccreative.co.uk
Embroidery thread available from stockists worldwide. Contact for stockists details

Needles, crochet hooks, ribbons, buttons etc available from needlework shops and haberdashery departments in department stores.

Mesh laundry bags, dolly balls and non slip matting available from household stores and household departments in department stores.

Index

ACKNOWLEDGEMENTS

My grateful thanks go to the following:

Connie Williamson at Jamieson & Smith (Shetland Wool Brokers Ltd), Gemma Saxon at Rowan, Sue Batley-Kyle and Jane Jubb at Sirdar, Jenny Thorpe and Karon Gillard at Twilleys of Stamford, and Juliet Sensicle and John Arbon at UK Alpaca for the generous yarn sponsorship.

The brilliant knitters: Alys Ackerman, Margaret Dayman, Kate Foster, Joyce Jackson and Nina Jackson. Sorry for all the late nights!

Sian Irvine for her perfect photographs. The wonderful children: Elena, Francesca, Maia, Lauren, Elliot and Leo who modelled the knits so beautifully.

Lisa Tai for designing the book, Sue Horan for checking the patterns and Mark Halstead for the garment diagrams.

Ruth Lyons for the garment sizes information. Cara Ackerman at DMC.

Rosemary Wilkinson for giving me this opportunity and all your help. Clare Sayer for all your hard work, support and enthusiasm.

My parents; Margaret and Martin Dayman and my sister; Kate Foster for providing everything from knitting expertise to childcare and plumbing in order to help!

My two sons; Elliot and Leo for being my models from day one, and being the best boys whilst I worked. And my husband Mark for your love, support and expert advice.